T0363275

Freshwater FISHES of Australia

by Bill Classon and Stephen Booth

Scientific editing by Paul Brown

Illustrations by Trevor Hawkins

First published in 2002 by
Australian Fishing Network

Australian Fishing Network Pty Ltd
PO Box 544, Croydon, VIC 3136
Tel: (03) 9729 8788
Fax: (03) 9729 7833
Email: sales@afn.com.au
Website: www.afn.com.au

Second Publication 2019

ISBN No. 9 781865 133355

INTRODUCTION

Australia is a dry island continent, and while our native freshwater species may not be as widespread and diverse as other countries, what species that do exist have evolved over thousands of years and become well adapted to our often harsh freshwater environment.

Since European settlement, many freshwater river, lakes and streams have been drastically altered for irrigation, navigation, flood mitigation and water storage. The construction of dams along our East Coast drainage rivers have had a profound detrimental effect.

Thankfully over the past couple of decades, communities, governments and their agencies, along with recreational anglers have realised the value of protecting and rehabilitating our waterways to protect and enhance native and introduced fish species, and at the same time re-establish fish species and populations into areas where they were locally extinct or vulnerable.

A number of native species are unique and excellent sportfish that recreational anglers are targeting for catch and release, and to a lesser extent, food. While at the same time, especially in the southern and eastern states, introduced species such as redfin, trout and salmon have adapted wonderfully well to many areas and also offer exceptional recreational angling.

This book has been produced to promote the diverse number of freshwater fish species, both native and introduced we have in Australia.

KEY

	Poor	Average	Good	Excellent
Eating	🍳	🍳🍳	🍳🍳🍳	🍳🍳🍳🍳
Sportfishing	🎣	🎣🎣	🎣🎣🎣	🎣🎣🎣🎣

POISONOUS

DO NOT EAT

PROTECTED

FORAGE

ENDANGERED

INTRODUCED

CONTENTS

ARCHER FISH

Scientific name: *Toxotes chatareus.* Also known as Rifle fish, Seven-spot archerfish.
Similar species: Gulf archer fish *Toxotes jaculatrix*, Western archer fish *Toxotes oligolepsis*,
Primitive archer fish *Toxotes lorentzi.*

Description: Laterally compressed body with a large, upturned mouth. Tail slightly forked and the dorsal fin with four spines set well back to enable the fish to sit in an upturned posture. Scales large and prominent, cover head and there are distinct black markings on the flanks.

Life cycle: Archer fish breed in fresh water and have established populations in artificial lakes where they have been introduced.

Conservation status: Archer fish are not currently endangered.

Fishing: Anglers use lures and flies to catch archer fish. An aggressive species, the archer fish will attack lures meant for much larger species and it is not uncommon for barramundi anglers to find an archer fish attached to their 15 cm long lure. Good fighters on light tackle, archer fish will readily take all standard trout lures and flies, including dry flies, and the species is often targeted by children who are enthralled by the species' eating habits.

Eating: It is not recommended that archer fish be taken as a table fish.

BARRAMUNDI

Scientific name: *Lates calcarifer.* Also known as Barra, Giant perch, Red eye, Pink eye.
Similar species: Nile perch (Africa) *Lates niloticus.*

Description: Barramundi have large scales, a big tail, a small head with a large mouth and heavy shoulders. Varying in colour from brilliant silver when in saltwater to very dark green/brown in fresh water, young barramundi often exhibit a prominent pale stripe down the head between the eyes.

With eyes that glow bright red/pink in torchlight, the barramundi has the name 'red eye' or 'pink eye' in some areas.

Life cycle: All barramundi start their lives as males and change sex to females as they mature. This sex change generally occurs when fish are between 55 and 75 cm long and after the age of five years. Spawning takes place in saltwater, with the young barramundi swimming upstream into fresh water lagoons and streams to grow.

Conservation status: The barramundi is not a threatened species, however, alteration to river flows and siltation of some rivers has reduced the available habitat for barramundi, especially in Queensland.

Fishing: Barramundi are the most popular sport fish found in Australia. This popularity stems from their attractive appearance, good fighting abilities and fine eating qualities. Barramundi are readily taken on trolled and cast lures, flies and baits, and can be located close to inflowing streams, rock bars, snags and depressions in the river bed. They are aggressive fish that will attack and eat almost anything small enough to fit in their mouth.

Eating: Barramundi are considered excellent fish for the table.

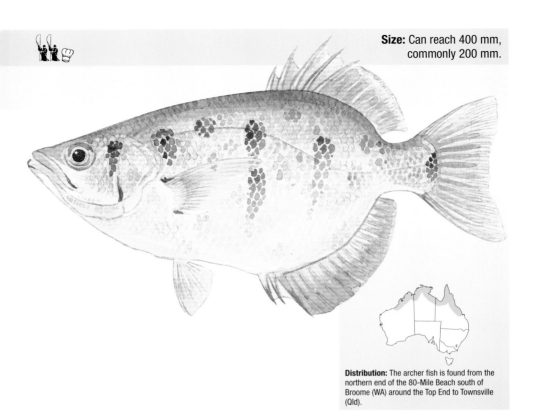

Distribution: The archer fish is found from the northern end of the 80-Mile Beach south of Broome (WA) around the Top End to Townsville (Qld).

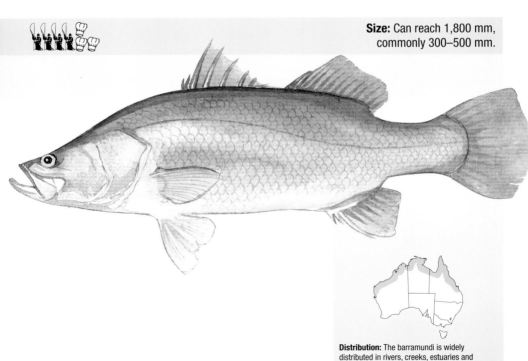

Distribution: The barramundi is widely distributed in rivers, creeks, estuaries and foreshores in the semi-tropical and tropical regions of Australia. Specimens have been taken from the Mary River (Qld) right around the Top End to Shark Bay (WA).

BASS, AUSTRALIAN

Scientific name: *Macquaria novemaculeata.* Also known as Perch.
Similar species: Estuary perch *Macquaria colonorum.*

Description: The Australian bass has a body that is elongate and compressed, with a snout profile that is slightly convex. The eyes and mouth are moderately large. The tail is slightly forked, the dorsal fin contains 8–11 spines and the anal fin contains 7–9 spines. A dark olive green on the back fading to off-white or yellowish in the gut, the fish can be very dark in colour. Anal and pelvic fins have white tips.

Life cycle: Australian bass are a catadromous species that migrate downstream to spawn in estuaries before migrating back upstream after breeding. Males mature at 2–4 years of age and approximately 180 mm of length. Females mature at 5–7 years of age and approximately 280 mm in length.

Bass have a high fecundity with an average of 440,000 eggs produced per female (this has been recorded up to 1.5 million eggs in individual fish).

Conservation status: Has severely declined in numbers as dams have restricted access to habitat both upstream and downstream. River regulation also interferes with breeding cycles. In recent years, the artificial breeding of fry and fingerling bass and subsequent release into large impoundments has seen the population explode.

Genetic integrity is a factor being considered in future stocking areas to ensure 'wild' populations are not affected by introduced genes, parasites and diseases from other catchments.

Fishing: Australian bass are a highly sought after recreational species. They fight exceptionally well for their size and are readily caught by a number of different methods. The species is arguably Australia's best light tackle freshwater sportfish.

All fishing methods are suitable for taking Australian bass, but they have become moretailored with the increasing popularity of these fish as a stocking option for impoundments. Most bass are commonly taken on trolled and cast lures; they are also readily taken on surface and sub-surface flies and live baits of shrimp, yabby and minnow.

Eating: Australian bass make excellent table fare, although most anglers choose to catch and release their fish. In rivers where natural populations are threatened, it is advisable not to take fish, but stocked impoundments provide a place for anglers to keep one or two fish for the table.

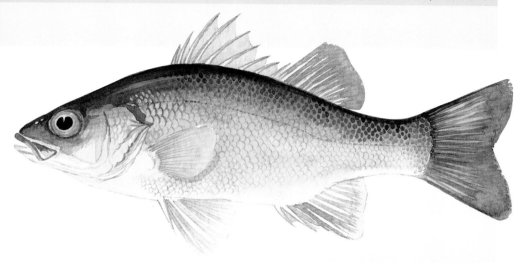

Distribution: Australian bass are distributed from Fraser Island and the Mary River in Queensland, south in all coastal draining rivers to Wilson's Promontory in Victoria. A stock enhancement population also exists in Lake Bullen Merri (Vic). Some individual fish have been recorded as far south as the Yarra River (Vic), but it is unlikely these fish are part of a breeding population and are more likely to have been stocked illegally. Another population is believed to exist in the upper Glenelg River (Vic), also from illegal liberation.

BLACKFISH, RIVER

Scientific name: *Gadopsis marmoratus.* Also known as Slippery, Slimey, Marbled cod.
Similar species: Two-spined blackfish *Gadopsis bispinosus.*

Description: River blackfish are an elongate and slender species with a large snout and mouth, with the upper jaw larger and protruding over the lower jaw. The dorsal fin contains 22–31 spines of which 6–13 are stout, and the anal fin contains 16–19 spines. The species has a rounded tail, small scales and its colour ranges from black to a brilliant white, green and brown that is marbled in appearance.

Life cycle: The life cycle is completed entirely in fresh water. Fecundity is low and eggs adhere to hollow logs and river substrate.

Conservation status: River management policies and snag removal have reduced the range of river blackfish and it is susceptible to increased sediment loads that are common in high use farming catchments.

Fishing: River blackfish are targeted in small creeks and streams that have a lot of woody cover and undercut banks. While most are commonly taken on worm or yabby baits, the species has been known to take a fly or lure around dusk when it roams from its home patch to feed. Casting lightly weighted baits near heavy structure or deep undercut banks is the best way to tempt a river blackfish.

Eating: River blackfish have a succulent white flesh that many people find delicious. Habitat loss and overfishing have reduced the population and catch-and-release fishing is recommended.

BLACKFISH, TWO-SPINED

Scientific name: *Gadopsis bispinosus.* Also known as River blackfish, Northern blackfish.
Similar species: River blackfish *Gadopsis marmoratus.*

Description: Two-spined blackfish are an elongate and slender species with a large snout and a mouth with a larger upper jaw protruding over the lower jaw. The species has a rounded tail, small scales and its colour ranges from black to a brilliant white, green and brown that is marbled in appearance.

Life cycle: The life cycle is completed entirely in fresh water. Fecundity is low and eggs adhere to hollow logs and river substrate. Two-spined blackfish have shown an ability to spawn in introduced PVC piping when habitat is limited.

Conservation status: An abundant species, two-spined blackfish has had its range reduced as a result of river management policies and snag removal, and it is susceptible to increased sediment loads that are common in high-use farming catchments.

Fishing: Sometimes caught in small creeks and streams with a lot of woody cover and undercut banks. The species is most commonly taken on worm or yabby baits, and when roaming from its home patch to feed at dusk, has been known to take a fly or lure.

Casting lightly weighted baits near heavy structure or deep undercut banks is the best way to tempt a river blackfish.

Eating: The fish's generally small size does not make it an appealing species to take for the table.

Distribution: River blackfish occur in many west-flowing streams in New South Wales and southern Queensland. They occur throughout Victoria on both sides of the Great Dividing Range and into South Australia as far west as the Murray River. The species is also found in Tasmania in the north, west and south-east coastal rivers.

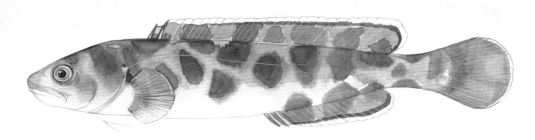

Distribution: Two-spined blackfish occur in streams north of the Great Dividing Range in north-eastern Victoria and south-eastern New South Wales.

BLUE-EYE, HONEY

Scientific name: *Pseudomugil mellis.*
Similar species: Southern blue-eye *Pseudomugil signifer.*

Description: A small fish with a large eye and small mouth. The scales are relatively large for the fish's size and are placed in even rows. Males and females display sexual dimorphism with males having extended first and second pelvic, dorsal and anal fins.

Life cycle: Honey blue-eye breed in fresh water and males vigorously guard nesting sites. Low fecundity in females reduces the number recruited in a breeding season. Young fish grow to maturity by three months.

Conservation status: This species has never been considered abundant and its habitat is rapidly being destroyed.

Fishing: Not considered a species of angling interest.

BLUE EYE, SOUTHERN

Scientific name: *Pseudomugil signifer.* Also known as Pacific blue eye, Common blue eye.
Similar species: Honey blue-eye *Pseudomugil mellis.*

Description: A small to mid sized fish with a large eye and small mouth. The scales are relatively large for the fish's size and are placed in even rows. Males and females display sexual dimorphism with males having extended first and second pelvic, dorsal and anal fins.

Life cycle: Honey blue-eye breed in fresh water and males guard nesting sites vigorously. Low fecundity in females reduces the number of fish recruited in a breeding season. Young fish grow to maturity by three months of age.

Conservation status: This species is abundant throughout its range, but is not found far inland.

Fishing: Not considered a species of angling interest.

BREAM, BONY

Scientific name: *Nematalosa erebi.* Also known as Melon fish, Pyberry and Tukari.
Similar species: Sometimes confused with smelt when small.

Description: A deep-bodied fish that is very compressed with a small head and a blunt snout. The species has 14–19 dorsal rays with the anterior ray being extended. The anal fin has 17–27 rays and the tail is forked. Colour varies from green on the back, fading to silver on the sides and white on the belly.

Life cycle: The bony bream spawns in spring after reaching maturity at the end of the first year, and at a size of approximately 80 mm. An omnivorous species, bony bream feed on detritus and algae, aquatic insects and small crustaceans.

Conservation status: The bony bream is currently under no threat.

Fishing: Bony bream are not targeted by anglers because of their small size, but they can be taken on small baits fished under floats in backwaters and slow flowing regions of the main water body.

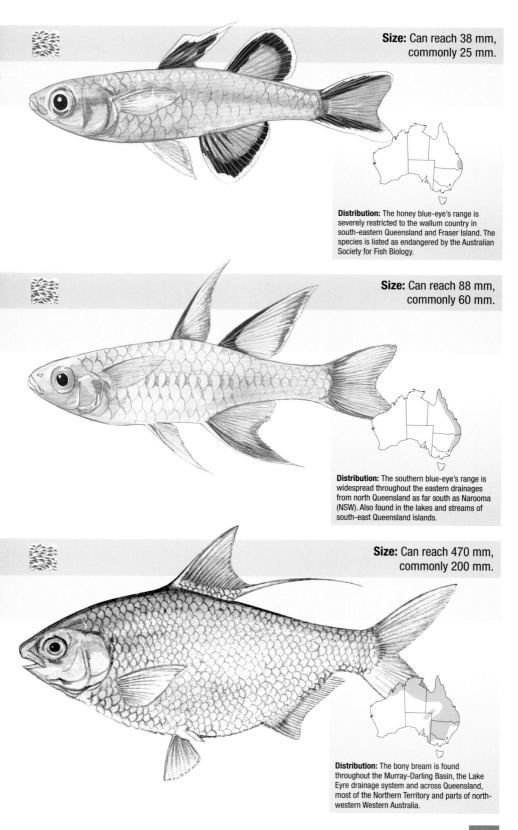

Size: Can reach 38 mm, commonly 25 mm.

Distribution: The honey blue-eye's range is severely restricted to the wallum country in south-eastern Queensland and Fraser Island. The species is listed as endangered by the Australian Society for Fish Biology.

Size: Can reach 88 mm, commonly 60 mm.

Distribution: The southern blue-eye's range is widespread throughout the eastern drainages from north Queensland as far south as Narooma (NSW). Also found in the lakes and streams of south-east Queensland islands.

Size: Can reach 470 mm, commonly 200 mm.

Distribution: The bony bream is found throughout the Murray-Darling Basin, the Lake Eyre drainage system and across Queensland, most of the Northern Territory and parts of north-western Western Australia.

BREAM, BLACK

Scientific name: *Acanthopagrus butcheri*. Also known as Blue nose bream, Southern bream.
Similar species: Yellowfin bream *Acanthopagrus australis*.

Description: Black bream are a robust and deep-bodied fish that is moderately compressed. Colour varies from an even gold/brown or bronze to a green/black on the back. Commonly the species has a darker head and more silver flanks. Belly colouration is milky white and the fins are dark. A single, long-based dorsal fin with hard spines and a terminal mouth with strong teeth are distinguishing features.

Life cycle: Black bream spawn between August and January at salinities between 11 and 18 per cent. The species is highly fecund with each female producing between one and three million eggs. Black bream mature at 3–4 years of age and their growth rate is slow. A 28 cm long fish is approximately eight years of age.

Conservation status: The black bream is under no immediate threat.

Fishing: Normally an estuary species, the black bream moves into the fresh water of coastal streams within its range. Bream are most commonly targeted with bait fixed to the bottom on a running sinker or paternoster rig. Best baits include sandworm, Bass yabbies, mussel, shrimp and small freshwater yabbies. Black bream can also be taken on lures and flies, with anglers targeting the species in thick snags and along reed lined banks.

Eating: Considered a delicacy by many anglers, the black bream is a popular table fish.

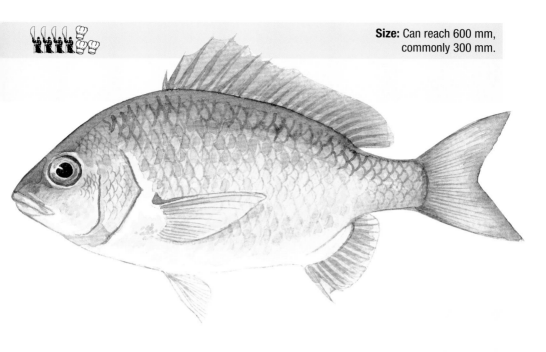

Size: Can reach 600 mm, commonly 300 mm.

Distribution: From Shark Bay (WA) around the southern coast to Mallacoota (Vic), including Tasmania. Black bream are rarely found in the sea, being most common in estuaries and freshwater rivers feeding estuaries.

BULLROUT

Scientific name: *Notesthes robusta.* Also known as Kroki.
Similar species: Fortescue *Centropogan australis.*

Description: A moderately sized and stocky fish, the bullrout is a superbly camouflaged species that has a mottled brown colouration that can change to suit the environment. The bullrout has poisonous spines along the dorsal surface that should be avoided by anglers. The pain from the poison is intense and medical treatment should be sought if the skin is punctured. Slight relief can be gained by placing the affected area in hot water to neutralise the protein structure of the poison.

Conservation status: This species is not considered threatened.

Fishing: Because of its poison spines and small size, anglers do not seek bullrout, however the flesh is tasty. Be aware that the poison is still active, even after the fish is dead.

CARP, COMMON

Scientific name: *Cyprinus carpio.* Also known as European carp, Euro, Crucian carp.
Similar species: Goldfish *Carassius auratus.*

Description: Carp are an elongated fish with a moderate head, small eyes and small mouth. The lips are thick with two barbels at each corner. The species is heavily scaled with colour varying from gold to olive green and silver. The dorsal fin stands erect and other fins tend to be darker in colour with some red marking on the anal fin and lower tail.

Common carp can also interbreed with goldfish to produce a sometimes-sterile hybrid offspring. These have smaller barbels, or no barbels at all, and share many features of both the common carp and the goldfish.

Life cycle: Some carp mature at one year of age and are ready to breed by age three. Females have a very high fecundity and each large female is typically able to produce up to one million eggs. Spawning occurs in spring when the water temperature reaches 17ºC, with a second spawning event occasionally occurring in late summer. Eggs are laid over aquatic or flooded vegetation and the young grow quickly in warm, plankton rich water.

Conservation status: Carp are an introduced exotic species that has very large populations throughout its range. It is considered a noxious pest in some states and must not be returned to the water.

Fishing: Carp can be taken by all angling methods and their hard and determined fight makes them appealing to many sportfishing anglers. Baits such as worms, grubs, shrimp, yabbies, corn and bread are favourites for carp angling, with more sporting anglers targeting the species with lures and flies. Carp are considered a noxious pest and must not be returned to the water alive. It is illegal to possess live carp in many Australian states.

Eating: Many cultures value carp highly as a table fish, however others believe carp to be muddy in taste.

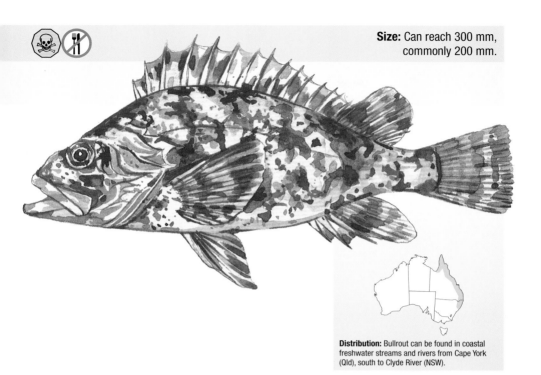

Size: Can reach 300 mm, commonly 200 mm.

Distribution: Bullrout can be found in coastal freshwater streams and rivers from Cape York (Qld), south to Clyde River (NSW).

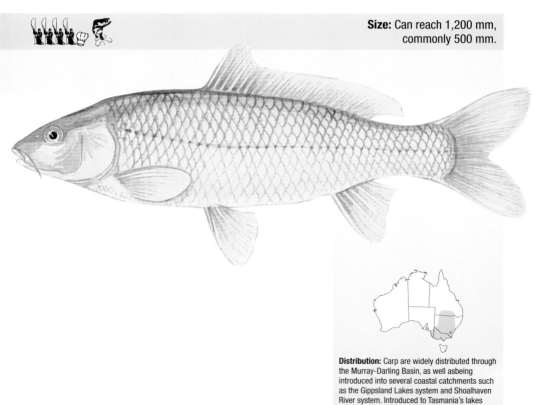

Size: Can reach 1,200 mm, commonly 500 mm.

Distribution: Carp are widely distributed through the Murray-Darling Basin, as well asbeing introduced into several coastal catchments such as the Gippsland Lakes system and Shoalhaven River system. Introduced to Tasmania's lakes Sorrell and Crescent in 1995, management efforts have reduced the numbers significantly, but not totally.

CATFISH, BLUE

Scientific name: *Arius graeffei*. Also known as Freshwater fork-tailed catfish.
Similar species: Salmon catfish *Arius leptuspis*, Lesser salmon catfish *Arius barneyi*.

Description: A tough skin with no scales covers a robust body with a broad, flattened head that is armoured for protection. Six barbels are located on the mouth, one on each upper corner and four on the lower lip. A spiny dorsal fin is placed high on the back and the species has a deeply forked tail. The serrated dorsal and pectoral spines can inflict painful wounds.

The colour varies from dark grey to dusky blue on the back, paling to silvery white on the belly.

Life cycle: The species is able to complete its entire life cycle in fresh water and breeding occurs from early November through to early December. Females spawn a small number of large eggs and thousands of smaller eggs. The developing eggs are incubated orally by the male for up to eight weeks. On hatching, the juveniles are maintained in the males' mouth until the yolk sack is absorbed.

Conservation status: Remains abundant throughout its range.

Fishing: Blue catfish and related similar species are readily taken on rod and reel by anglers fishing the northern half of Australia. They provide reasonable sport and can occasionally be taken on lures and flies.

Eating: The flesh is reasonable eating, although some claim (incorrectly) the flesh is poisonous.

CATFISH, CENTRAL AUSTRALIAN

Scientific name: *Neosilurus argenteus*.
Similar species: Hyrtl's tandan *Neosilurus hyrtlii*.

Description: An elongated species with a tapering tail and small head terminating with a small mouth, which is surrounded by four pairs of barbels. Stout, serrated dorsal spine and pectoral spines are poisonous and should be avoided. Body colour is silvery white with orange fins.

Life cycle: Very little is known of the life history of this fish.

Conservation status: Abundant throughout its natural range.

Fishing: Very little angler interest due to its size and poisonous spines.

Distribution: Found in coastal drainages from northern New South Wales through Queensland and Northern Territory to the far west coast of Western Australia.

Distribution: Occurs in inland rivers of South Australia and Northern Territory, as well as rivers entering the Gulf of Carpentaria.

CATFISH, EEL-TAILED

Scientific name: *Tandanus tandanus.* Also known as Tandan, Freshwater jewfish.
Similar species: Toothless catfish *Anodontiglanis dahli*, Black catfish *Neosiluris ater*, Freshwater cobbler *Tandanus bostocki.*

Description: Eel-tailed catfish have a stout, robust body that is compressed towards the tail. Eyes of moderate size sit on a large, ventrally flattened head that is terminated with thick, fleshy lips lined with four pairs of barbels. First dorsal fin is erect and preceded by a serrated spine while the second dorsal fin extends through to the tail. Dorsal and pectoral fins are poisonous, although less so as the individual becomes larger. Skin is smooth and tough with no scales.

Smaller fish are mottled in appearance while larger fish tend to be dark brown or black, fading to whitish below.

Life cycle: Catfish build a nest between 0.5 and 2 metres in diameter where the female lays her eggs as the male fertilises them. Young grow reasonably quickly reaching 90 mm by their first winter. Most catfish will remain near the one location for their entire lives.

Conservation status: Catfish are considered rare in many parts of the Murray-Darling, but they have developed strong populations in many artificial lakes and impoundments.

Fishing: Fishing after dark is a great way to catch an eel-tailed catfish. They readily take worms, shrimps, yabbies and grubs intended for other species. The species occasionally takes lures, especially in clear water impoundments when they are run near weed beds in shallow water. Eel-tailed catfish are strong fighters that are worthy adversaries on light line.

Eating: Their flesh is clean and quite tasty.

CICHLID, BLACK MANGROVE

Scientific name: *Tilapia mariae.* Also known as Nigger cichlid.
Similar species: Convict cichlid *Cichlasoma nigrofasciatum.*

Description: All cichlids in Australia have a strongly compressed body that is ovate in shape. The species has a small mouth and a relatively large eye with a single dorsal fin that has 12–15 spines and an anal fin with 10–12 rays. Colour pattern changes with size; small fish are olive green with 7–8 vertical bands; large fish are lightish yellow with the vertical banding being less distinct and 6–8 prominent spots.

Life cycle: Lays eggs on clean sites and parents guard eggs ferociously. Parental care continues until fry reach 25 mm.

Conservation status: Introduced exotic species native to Africa.

Fishing: Only recognised as an aquarium species.

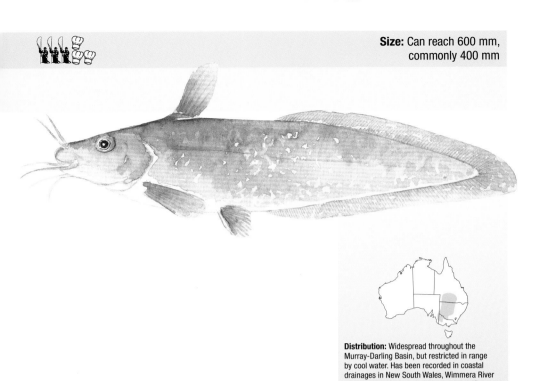

Distribution: Widespread throughout the Murray-Darling Basin, but restricted in range by cool water. Has been recorded in coastal drainages in New South Wales, Wimmera River (Vic) and Queensland, but current scientific studies suggest these are transplanted species, or separate sub-species.

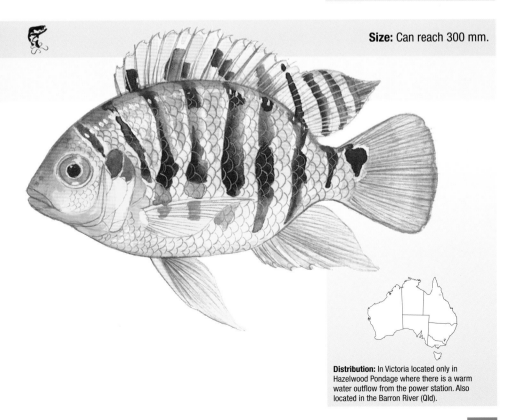

Size: Can reach 300 mm.

Distribution: In Victoria located only in Hazelwood Pondage where there is a warm water outflow from the power station. Also located in the Barron River (Qld).

CICHLID, CONVICT

Scientific name: *Cichlasoma nigrofasciatum*. Also known as Zebra cichlid.
Similar species: Black mangrove cichlid *Tilapia mariae*.

Description: Strongly compressed body that is ovate in shape. Small mouth and relatively large eye with a single dorsal fin having 7–8 spines while the anal fin has six rays. Dorsal surface is dark grey to bluish black, sides often with a violet sheen and the belly fades to pale grey. Adults have 8–9 vertical bands and females are generally duller in colour than males.

Life cycle: Lays eggs on clean sites and parents guard eggs ferociously. Parental care continues until fry reach 25 mm.

Conservation status: Introduced exotic species native to Central and South America.

Fishing: Only recognised as an aquarium species.

COD, EASTERN FRESHWATER

Scientific name: *Maccullochella ikei*. Also known as Clarence River cod, East Coast cod, Eastern cod.
Similar species: Murray cod *Maccullochella peelii peelii*, Trout cod *Maccullochella macquariensis*, Mary River cod, *Maccullochella peelii mariensis*.

Description: A large, elongate fish with relatively small eyes and a distinctive concave head profile. Yellow green to golden with black to very dark green mottling. Pale green to white margins on fins and cream to white belly. Has been recorded up to 41 kg, but commonly only up to 5 kg.

Life cycle: Little is known, but believed to breed at five years of age between 0.7 and 1.5 kg. Spawning takes place when water temperature reaches 16ºC.

Conservation status: Eastern freshwater cod are considered endangered and have become extinct in the Richmond and Brisbane rivers. Now being bred in hatcheries, the Eastern freshwater cod is being reintroduced into these waterways. Mining and bushfire related pollution, loss of habitat due to railway construction and agricultural development are thought to be responsible for the decline of the species. Listed as endangered by the Australian Society of Fish Biology.

Fishing: Eastern freshwater cod are a protected species and may not be deliberately targeted by anglers.

Size: Can reach 150 mm.

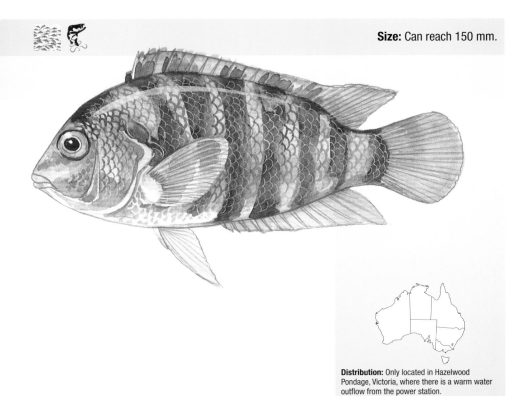

Distribution: Only located in Hazelwood Pondage, Victoria, where there is a warm water outflow from the power station.

Size: Can reach 1,200 mm, commonly 550 mm.

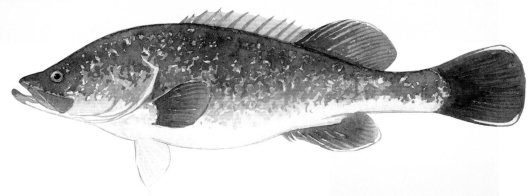

Distribution: Eastern freshwater cod are only found in the Clarence and Richmond rivers of New South Wales.

COD, MARY RIVER

Scientific name: *Maccullochella peelii mariensis.* Also known as Queensland cod.
Similar species: Murray cod *Maccullochella peelii peelii,* Trout cod *Maccullochella macquariensis,* Eastern freshwater cod, *Maccullochella ikei.*

Description: A large, elongate fish with relatively small eyes with a distinctive concave head profile. Yellow green to golden with black to very dark green mottling over the body with pale green to white margins on fins and cream to white on the belly. The pelvic fin filaments are longer than those in other cod species and are a diagnostic feature. The species has been recorded up to 23 kg, but commonly only up to 5 kg.

Life cycle: Little is known, but believed to breed at five years of age. Spawning takes place when water temperature reaches 20ºC.

Conservation status: Mary River cod are considered endangered and are restricted to only five small tributaries of the Mary River. Loss of habitat due to urban expansion and agricultural development are factors in their decline. The species is listed as critically endangered by the Australian Society for Fish Biology.

Fishing: Mary River cod are a protected species and may not be targeted deliberately by anglers.

COD, MURRAY

Scientific name: *Maccullochella peelii peelii.* Also known as Goodoo, Green fish.
Similar species: Eastern freshwater cod *Maccullochella ikei,* Trout cod *Maccullochella macquariensis,* Mary River cod, *Maccullochella peelii mariensis.*

Description: A large, elongate fish with relatively small eyes with a distinctive concave head profile. Creamy-olive green to yellow green to golden with black to very dark green mottling over the body with pale green to white margins on fins and cream to white belly. Adults have very few marks on their heads. Murray cod have been recorded up to 113 kg, but commonly only up to 5 kg.

Life cycle: Murray cod reach maturity at 4–5 years of age and spawn in spring and early summer when water temperatures rise above 20ºC. Murray cod are known to make long distance migration in preparation for breeding, and after breeding, return to the same snag from where they started.

Conservation status: Murray cod are considered to be threatened, but not endangered at present. Numbers have declined dramatically in the wild due to overharvesting, river improvements and especially cold water releases from dams. The species is very successfully bred in hatcheries and released across its range.

Fishing: Murray cod are considered the prize catch for inland anglers. They can be targeted on baits, lures or flies and the variety of habitats in which Murray cod are found make them a relatively easy species to target. Fishing near deep holes with snags or structure such as rocks, fallen trees, weed beds and clay banks should ensure success.

Eating: The flesh of Murray cod is very fatty and undesirable in larger specimens, however fish up to 5 kg are excellent eating.

PROTECTED

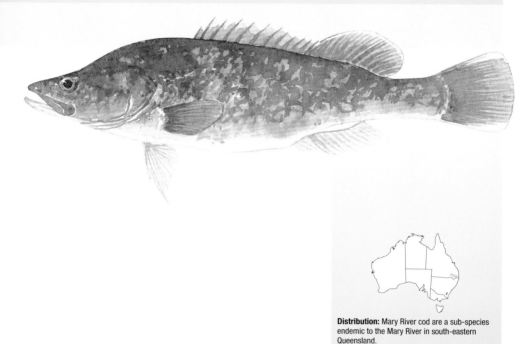

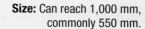

Distribution: Mary River cod are a sub-species endemic to the Mary River in south-eastern Queensland.

Size: Can reach 1,800 mm, commonly 500 mm.

Distribution: Murray cod are found throughout the entire Murray-Darling Basin, except for some cold water, high altitude tributaries and cold tail-races below large dams. There is also a self-sustaining population in the Nepean River (NSW) and Yarra River (Vic), which is enhanced by illegal stocking.

COD, TROUT

Scientific name: *Maccullochella macquariensis.* Also known as Blue nose, Blue cod.
Similar species: Eastern freshwater cod *Maccullochella ikei*, Murray cod *Maccullochella peelii peelii*, Mary River cod *Maccullochella peelii mariensis.*

Description: A large, elongate fish with relatively small eyes with a distinctive straight to concave head profile. Coloration is commonly bluish grey with black to very dark green spots across the flanks continuing onto the head with the ventral surface being creamy white to grey. Trout cod have been recorded up to 16 kg, but are more commonly seen up to 2 kg in weight.

Life cycle: Little is known, but believed to breed at five years of age between 0.7 and 1.5 kg. Spawning takes place in spring when water temperature reaches 18ºC.

Conservation status: Trout cod are endangered throughout their entire range and listed by the Australian Society for Fish Biology as critically endangered.

Fishing: Listed under the Victorian Flora and Fauna Guarantee Act 1988 and may not be targeted or taken by anglers.

CONGOLLI

Scientific name: *Pseudaphritis urvillii.* Also known as Tupong, Sand trout, Sandy.
Similar species: Unlikely to be confused with any other species in freshwater.

Description: A small to medium sized fish with an almost cylindrical body shape and conical head that is flattened on top with small eyes. The lower jaw is longer than the top jaw. Colour is variable depending on substrate, but mostly greenish brown on back, irregularly marked on the side to a uniform yellowish colour on the ventral surface.

Life cycle: Little is known of the breeding, but the congolli is believed to breed in saltwater in autumn and winter.

Conservation status: Remains widespread and abundant throughout its range.

Fishing: Not specifically targeted by anglers, however can be caught on small hooks with worm or shrimp baits intended for other species. Its small size means it is rarely taken for the table, but it is considered to have good eating flesh.

PROTECTED

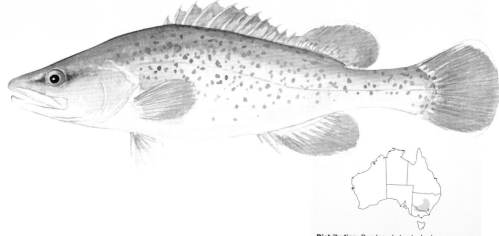

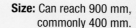

Distribution: Due largely to stocked reintroductions, trout cod are found throughout the southern tributaries of the Murray River, although their range has been limited by dams, weirs and flood mitigation works. There are no confirmed reports of trout cod existing in the Darling River. The population that exists in the mid-Murray River between Barmah and Yarrawonga is the only naturally breeding remnant population of the original, pre-European stock.

Size: Can reach 340 mm, commonly 150 mm.

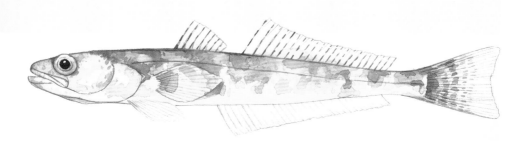

Distribution: Congolli are common in coastal freshwater streams from the Murray River (SA) through to Bega River (NSW), including Tasmania.

EEL, LONG FINNED

Scientific name: *Anguilla reinhardtii.* Also known as Freshwater eel, Conger eel.
Similar species: Short finned eel *Anguilla australis.*

Description: Closely resembles short finned eel but has the dorsal fin beginning well in front of the anal fin. Broad head with thick, fleshy lips and a large mouth extending well past the eyes. Distinctly blotched or mottled on the dorsal surface, fading to a creamy white on the belly.

Life cycle: Believed to spawn in the Coral Sea, the young are transported on ocean currents before changing into glass eels near the Australian coast and swimming vast distances up river as elvers. In the rivers, the eel can spend up to 10 years growing before returning to the spawning grounds. Eels can also travel over moist ground to colonise new waterways.

Conservation status: The long finned eel is abundant across its range.

Fishing: Baits such as yabbies, worms, fish gut and grubs can be fished on the bottom with a running sinker rig. Best times are at dusk and into the night. Long finned eels fight hard with a characteristic back swimming action that can see the eel escape into a snag very quickly.

Eating: Long finned eel's flesh is very palatable, although oily.

EEL, SHORT FINNED

Scientific name: *Anguilla australis.* Also known as Silver eel.
Similar species: Long finned eel *Anguilla reinhardtii.*

Description: Elongate and cylindrical with continuous dorsal, caudal and anal fins that are soft. The dorsal and anal fins originate at a similar point down the body. Broad head with thick, fleshy lips and a large mouth extending well past the eyes. The scales are indistinct and colour varies from a light tan to dark brown on the dorsal surface fading to a creamy white on the belly.

Life cycle: Believed to spawn in the Coral Sea, the young are transported on ocean currents before changing into glass eels off the coast and swimming vast distances up river as brown pigmented elvers. In the rivers the eels can spend up to 20 years growing before returning to the spawning grounds. Eels can also travel over moist ground to colonise new waterways.

Conservation status: The short finned eel remains abundant across its range.

Fishing: Baits such as yabbies, worms and grubs can be fished on the bottom with a running sinker rig. Best times are at dusk and into the night. Short finned eels fight hard with a characteristic back swimming action that can see the eel escape into a snag very quickly.

Eating: Short finned eel's flesh is also very palatable.

Size: Can reach 1,650 mm, commonly 1,000 mm.

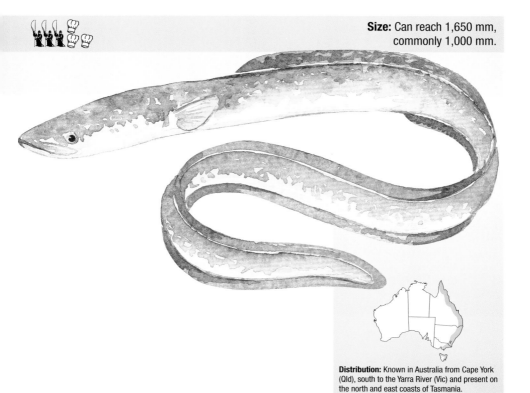

Distribution: Known in Australia from Cape York (Qld), south to the Yarra River (Vic) and present on the north and east coasts of Tasmania.

Size: Can reach 1,100 mm, commonly 500 mm.

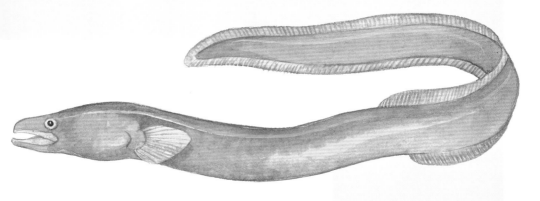

Distribution: Known in Australia from Caboolture River (Qld), south to the vicinity of Mount Gambier (SA), including the north-west, northern and eastern coasts of Tasmania.

EMPIREFISH

Scientific name: *Hypseleotris compressa*. Also known as Carp gudgeon, Empire gudgeon.
Similar species: Firetailed gudgeon *Hypseleotris galii,* Western carp gudgeon *Hypseleotris klunzingeri*.

Description: A small species, its body is very compressed and elongate. Males grow larger than females and develop a slight hump on their heads. The colour varies considerably and individuals can rapidly darken or lighten to blend with its current environment. A series of striated stripes are present across the dorsal and anal fins, as well as a series of white spots on the second dorsal.

Life cycle: Empirefish mature at 40–50 mm and spawning occurs in the warmer months. Juveniles develop in estuaries. Females often spawn several times a year and one female may spawn with many different males.

Conservation status: The species is relatively common throughout its range.

Fishing: This species is too small for any angler interest.

GALAXIAS, CLARENCE

Scientific name: *Galaxias johnstoni*.
Similar species: Climbing galaxias *Galaxias brevipinnis,* Pedder galaxias *Galaxias pedderensis,* Mountain galaxias *Galaxias olidus*.

Description: A moderately stout species with a blunt head, the Clarence galaxias has small fins and a truncated tail. Colour is dark greyish brown on back and sides, silvery olive below with bold, irregular brownish bands and blotches on sides.

Life cycle: Spawns during spring following migration into flowing water. The species lives its entire four year life in fresh water.

Conservation status: Range reduced in recent years to the extent the species is listed as critically endangered by the Australian Society for Fish Biology.

Fishing: Not allowed to be collected or used as bait.

GALAXIAS, CLIMBING

Scientific name: *Galaxias brevipinnis*. Also known as Cox's mountain galaxid.
Similar species: Mountain galaxias *Galaxias olidus*, Pedder galaxias *Galaxias pedderensis,* Clarence galaxias *Galaxias johnstoni*.

Description: A relatively large and elongate species that has an almost tubular trunk. Large mouth with a clearly shorter lower jaw. Fins are thick and fleshy. Greyish brown to dark olive on back, paling on sides. Often has a distinct blue-black splotch above the pectoral fin base. Belly a dull silvery olive with a gold iridescence evident in bright sunlight.

Life cycle: Very little is known, but believed to have the ability to spawn in fresh water, with the young being swept to sea before returning to the streams and lakes.

Conservation status: Distribution has been fragmented from deforestation and the introduction of rainbow and brown trout. Not presently endangered, but could be at risk locally.

Fishing: The climbing galaxias is part of the valuable Tasmanian whitebait fishery where they are netted with many other galaxias species. They are used as live or dead bait to fish for the large sea-run trout that follow the migrating schools into the estuaries. Note that live bait is not allowed to be used in inland waters of Tasmania.

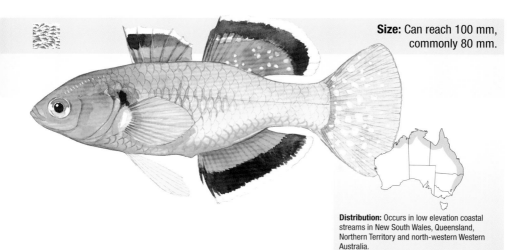

Size: Can reach 100 mm, commonly 80 mm.

Distribution: Occurs in low elevation coastal streams in New South Wales, Queensland, Northern Territory and north-western Western Australia.

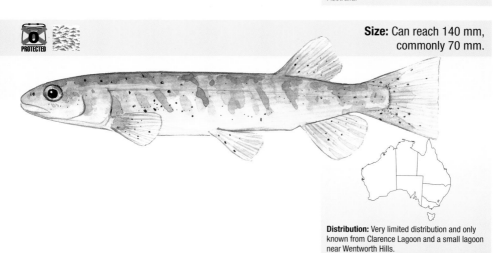

Size: Can reach 140 mm, commonly 70 mm.

Distribution: Very limited distribution and only known from Clarence Lagoon and a small lagoon near Wentworth Hills.

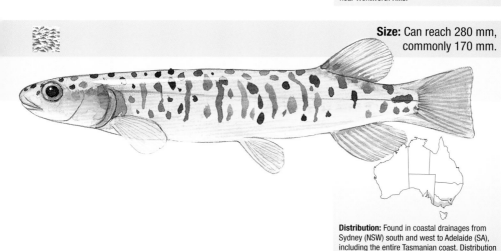

Size: Can reach 280 mm, commonly 170 mm.

Distribution: Found in coastal drainages from Sydney (NSW) south and west to Adelaide (SA), including the entire Tasmanian coast. Distribution is believed to be fragmented across the range due to habitat loss. Also found in the upper Murray River where it is believed to have arrived with water transferred from the Snowy River Drainage as part of the Snowy Hydro Scheme.

GALAXIAS, EASTERN LITTLE

Scientific name: *Galaxiella pusilla*. Also known as Dwarf galaxias.
Similar species: Unlike any other fishes within its range.

Description: A tiny, stocky fish with a short snout and small fins. A rounded tail and large eye are distinguishing features. A transparent olive-amber stripe on back with three black stripes along the trunk although colour varies between the sexes. The difference is the male has a brilliant orange stripe between the middle and lower black stripe, which the female lacks.

Life cycle: Occurs mostly in still or slow flowing water that is heavily overgrown with aquatic vegetation. Can exist in water that dries in warmer months by utilising yabby holes to aestivate (spend warmer months in a state of inactivity).

Conservation status: Distribution fragmented due to wetland drainage and is listed as vulnerable by the Australian Society for Fish Biology.

Fishing: Not recommended as an angling or bait species due to low numbers.

GALAXIAS, GOLDEN

Scientific name: *Galaxias auratus*.
Similar species: Spotted galaxias *Galaxias truttaceus*.

Description: A large, stout-bodied species with a long head and slender snout. A large mouth with moderate eye and thick, fleshy fins. Gold to olive on back paling to bronze on the flanks and silver grey on belly. Juveniles have characteristic grey-olive bands, which fragment in adults to round and oval spots.

Life cycle: Is a species of still and slow flowing waters. Life cycle is fully completed in fresh water with spawning in spring.

Conservation status: Remains in high abundance, but the effect of carp and trout is not yet fully understood. The species is listed as endangered by the Australian Society for Fish Biology due to its limited distribution.

Fishing: The species is an important forage species for trout, but may not be collected and used for bait in inland waters of Tasmania.

GALAXIAS, MOUNTAIN

Scientific name: *Galaxias olidus*. Also known as Inland galaxias.
Similar species: Climbing galaxias *Galaxias brevipinnis*, Barred galaxias *Galaxias fuscus*.

Description: A small and stout galaxias with a small head and blunt snout. Fins are small, thick and fleshy. Widely variable colour from yellowish green on the back to brown, fading to an olive or silvery white belly. The back and upper sides are profusely covered with speckling, blotches and banding or bars.

Life cycle: Completes its entire life cycle in fresh water and spawns in spring with females producing few eggs (only up to 350 for an 80 mm long specimen). Young move in loose shoals until finding suitable habitat. There is no sea-going phase during maturity.

Conservation status: Remains locally abundant and widespread in its natural range, but does suffer from predation by trout and redfin, both species capable of making the mountain galaxias locally extinct, although sometimes mountain galaxias coexist with trout by hiding in the cobbles of the stream bed.

Fishing: Not large enough to interest anglers, but very occasionally taken on tiny dry and wet flies by fly fishers in small water.

Size: Females grow to 40 mm and males only to 34 mm.

Distribution: Found in southern Victoria from Gippsland west to the eastern corner of South Australia. Also present on Flinders Island and the north-east coast of Tasmania.

Size: Can reach 230 mm, commonly 140 mm.

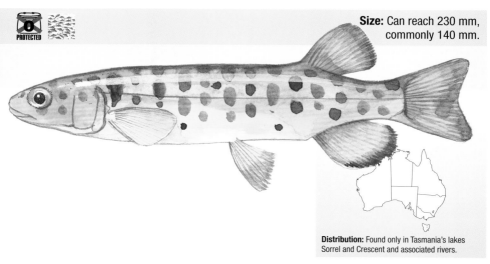

Distribution: Found only in Tasmania's lakes Sorrel and Crescent and associated rivers.

Size: Can attain a length of 135 mm, commonly 70 mm.

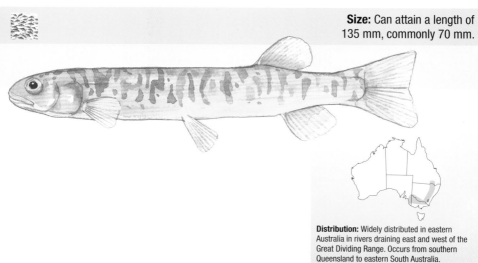

Distribution: Widely distributed in eastern Australia in rivers draining east and west of the Great Dividing Range. Occurs from southern Queensland to eastern South Australia.

GALAXIAS, PEDDER

Scientific name: *Galaxias pedderensis.*
Similar species: Climbing galaxias *Galaxias brevipinnis*, Clarence galaxias *Galaxias johnstoni*, Swan galaxias *Galaxias fontanus.*

Description: The Pedder galaxias is a more slender and elongate galaxias with a strongly depressed head. Greenish brown in colour, the sides are covered with brownish and off-white contrasting bands and blotches. A golden iridescence is visible in some lighting conditions.

Life cycle: Very little is known about the species. Becomes sexually mature at two years of age and may live for six years.

Conservation status: Extremely rare in its natural environment. Considered the rarest fish species in fresh water. The species is listed as critically endangered by the Australian Society for Fish Biology.

Fishing: Can not take or use as bait in any water.

GALAXIAS, SADDLED

Scientific name: *Galaxias tanycephalus.*
Similar species: Confusion is unlikely with other galaxias.

Description: A stout-bodied species reaching a moderate size with a long head, slender snout and equal length jaws. The well developed fins are thick and fleshy and a forked tail of moderate length is distinctive. The colour is green olive on the back with saddle-like grey bars or spots across the back and sides with a silvery belly and olive fins.

Life cycle: Not well known, but is found in bouldery debris around lake margins. Entire life cycle is in fresh water.

Conservation status: Never found to be abundant and considered vulnerable in its natural range.

Fishing: Can not be collected or used as bait in Tasmanian waters.

GALAXIAS, SPOTTED

Scientific name: *Galaxias truttaceus.* Also known as Spotted mountain galaxid, Spotted trout.
Similar species: Golden galaxias *Galaxias auratus*, Saddled galaxias *Galaxias tanycephalus.*

Description: A large and stout-bodied species that is deep bellied with a broad and deep head and a large mouth that has equal length jaws. Fins quite large and rounded, and the tail is slightly forked. Brownish to deep olive in colour, this fades to brownish grey on the sides, turning silvery on the belly. The trunk is covered with many round spots that sometimes appear in vertical rows. A distinct diagonal stripe passes back and down through the eye.

Life cycle: A low elevation species with riverine populations spawning in late winter and landlocked populations spawning in spring. At 140 mm in length, females can lay up to 16,000 eggs. Riverine populations have a saltwater migratory stage with juveniles returning as whitebait.

Conservation status: Remains locally abundant but range fragmented through deforestation.

Fishing: Forms part of the valuable whitebait fishery in Tasmania and is used in Victoria as a live bait for trout, estuary perch and bream.

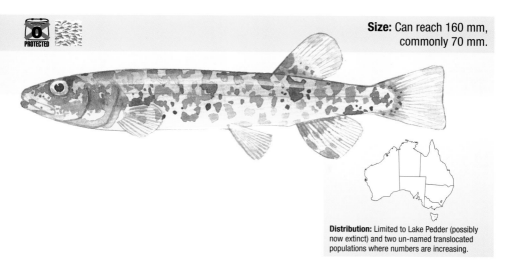

Size: Can reach 160 mm, commonly 70 mm.

Distribution: Limited to Lake Pedder (possibly now extinct) and two un-named translocated populations where numbers are increasing.

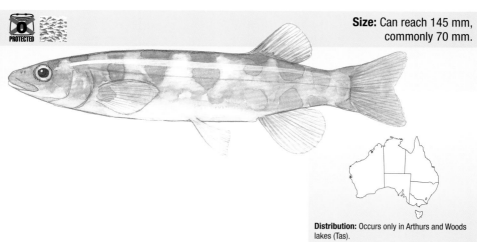

Size: Can reach 145 mm, commonly 70 mm.

Distribution: Occurs only in Arthurs and Woods lakes (Tas).

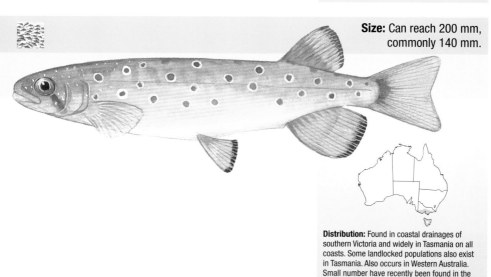

Size: Can reach 200 mm, commonly 140 mm.

Distribution: Found in coastal drainages of southern Victoria and widely in Tasmania on all coasts. Some landlocked populations also exist in Tasmania. Also occurs in Western Australia. Small number have recently been found in the Campaspe River (Vic) probably originating from illegal introduction.

GALAXIAS, SWAMP

Scientific name: *Galaxias parvus*. Also known as Dwarf galaxia.
Similar species: Unlikely to be confused with other species

Description: A small fish with a tubular trunk tapering to a long caudal peduncle. A small mouth adorns a moderate head with moderate sized eyes. Back and sides are greyish yellow becoming grey green on lower sides and whitish on belly. Back and sides have numerous small and irregular dark spots and blotches.

Life cycle: The species is found in swamps, pools and backwaters amongst vegetation and boulders. Males mature at one year of age; females at age two and the species can complete its life cycle entirely in fresh water.

Conservation status: Became more abundant with the construction of Lake Pedder and remains abundant, but is listed as data deficient by the Australian Society for Fish Biology.

Fishing: Cannot be collected or used as bait in Tasmanian waters.

GALAXIAS, SWAN

Scientific name: *Galaxias fontanus*.
Similar species: Clarence galaxias *Galaxias olidus*, Mountain galaxias *Galaxias johnstoni*.

Description: A moderate sized species with a flattened head and a slightly forked tail. All fins are fleshy and without markings. Colour varies from brownish olive on back and sides covered with dense and irregular brown blotching to a belly that is silvery white.

Life cycle: Completes its whole life cycle in fresh water and is the only galaxid endemic to Tasmania's east coast. Lives for at least three years, spawning at age two.

Conservation status: The species is listed as critically endangered by the Australian Society for Fish Biology in its natural range and is heavily preyed upon by brown trout when juvenile.

Fishing: Cannot be collected or used as bait in Tasmanian waters.

GAMBUSIA, EASTERN

Scientific name: *Gambusia holbrooki*. Also known as Mosquito fish.
Similar species: Guppy *Poecilia reticulata*.

Description: A small fish with a deep rounded belly. The lower jaw a little larger than bottom the jaw. Females are distinctly larger than males and have a representative black spot above the vent, forward of the anal fin. Generally greenish olive on back, the belly is silver white and smaller individuals may appear translucent.

Life cycle: Gambusia tolerate a wide range of environmental conditions and can reproduce rapidly, up to nine times a year, when conditions are suitable. Young are live born and can mature in as little as two months.

Conservation status: An introduced exotic species that is aggressive and has been known to displace and out-compete native fish species, frogs and tadpoles. Classed as noxious in Victoria.

Fishing: Offers little interest to anglers. Can not be used as a live bait in Victoria.

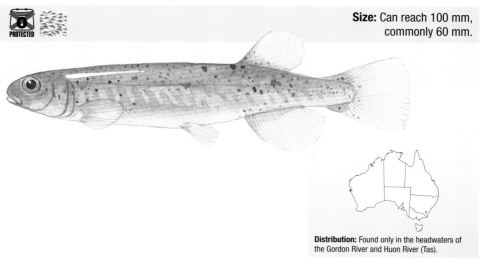

Size: Can reach 100 mm, commonly 60 mm.

Distribution: Found only in the headwaters of the Gordon River and Huon River (Tas).

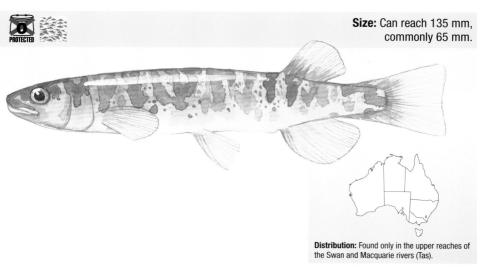

Size: Can reach 135 mm, commonly 65 mm.

Distribution: Found only in the upper reaches of the Swan and Macquarie rivers (Tas).

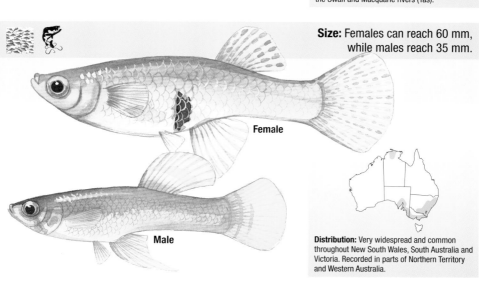

Size: Females can reach 60 mm, while males reach 35 mm.

Female

Male

Distribution: Very widespread and common throughout New South Wales, South Australia and Victoria. Recorded in parts of Northern Territory and Western Australia.

GARFISH, RIVER

Scientific name: *Hyporhamphus regularis.*
Similar species: Sea garfish *Hyporhamphus melanochir.*

Description: River garfish have a stout body with a detectable silver stripe running down the side. Large scales with a generally dull beak colour with the upper jaw being more broad than long. Colour grades from green blue on top to silver on sides and silver white on belly.

Life cycle: Spends the majority of its life in estuaries attaching its eggs to aquatic plants with fine tendrils. Has been recorded up to 200 km inland from the sea.

Conservation status: This species is abundant throughout its range.

Fishing: Can be caught using light tackle and small hooks. Baits such as maggots, pieces of peeled prawn and marine worms are excellent. Suspend baits below a float, or use them unweighted to get the best results. Rarely taken on fly tackle, but this is an option.

Eating: River garfish make excellent food but are full of small bones.

GARFISH, SNUB NOSED

Scientific name: *Arrhamphus sclerolepis.*
Similar species: Should not be confused with any other garfish due to its unique appearance.

Description: The snub nosed garfish differs in appearance to other garfish in that the lower jaw is only about one fifth the length of the head. Tail is deeply forked. The lower jaw also has a prominent red tip. Olive on the back, fading to silver on the sides and white on the belly.

Life cycle: Snub nosed garfish can maintain populations in freshwater environments, but most commonly breed in saltwater. Eggs are pelagic.

Conservation status: Snub nosed garfish are abundant throughout its range and where they have been artificially introduced.

Fishing: Snub nosed garfish will take small baits such as worms, maggots and peeled prawn fished under floats on light line rigs. Berley helps to attract and hold a school of garfish in the fishing area.

Eating: Snub nosed garfish are thicker than most garfish and make excellent eating.

GOBY, BLUE SPOTTED

Scientific name: *Pseudogobius* sp.
Similar species: Swan River goby *Pseudogobius olorum*, Tasmanian goby *Tasmanogobius lordii.*

Description: A small, cylindrical goby with a small mouth that is commonly overhung by a plump snout. Mature females tend to have a larger, more rounded belly than males. Head and body light brown with a dull pearly white belly. Live fish appear to have a goldish fleck across the flanks. Flanks covered with dark blotches that may be more prominent in mature males.

Life cycle: Little is known, but believed to spawn in the upper reaches of estuaries where low salinities occur. Able to tolerate fresh water, but rarely encountered far from estuaries.

Conservation status: Remains common throughout its range

Fishing: Rarely seen or targeted by anglers. May have some use as a live bait in certain areas where allowed.

Size: Can reach 350 mm, commonly 300 mm.

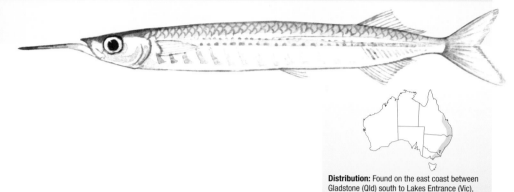

Distribution: Found on the east coast between Gladstone (Qld) south to Lakes Entrance (Vic), and on the west coast from Bunbury (WA) to Kalbarri (WA).

Size: Can reach a length of 380 mm.

Distribution: Distributed from Carnarvon (WA), north and across the Top End to northern New South Wales. Has been stocked into some inland lakes and impoundments.

Size: Can grow to 45 mm, commonly 35 mm.

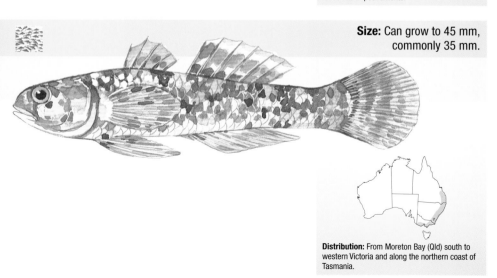

Distribution: From Moreton Bay (Qld) south to western Victoria and along the northern coast of Tasmania.

GOBY, BRIDLED

Scientific name: *Amoya bifrenatus*.
Similar species: Is unlike other freshwater gobies.

Description: A slightly compressed head with a broadly rounded snout is characterised by bulbous cheeks. Small and elongate, the tail is also elongated to the point of becoming pointed in males. The head and body are pale grey to light brown, with a short black bar above the mouth. A series of bluey green iridescent spots can often be seen scattered over the head. Fins vary in colour, but have distinctive black stripes.

Life cycle: Prefers mud and sand bottoms where it seeks shelter in burrows. Lives for 3–4 years and attaches spawned eggs to objects on the bottom or in burrows.

Conservation status: Common in its natural range, but rare in fresh water.

Fishing: Too small to be of interest to anglers except as a bait fish where allowed.

GOBY, CONCAVE

Scientific name: *Glossogobius concavifrons*.
Similar species: Other *Glossogobius* species.

Description: Elongate with a rounded tail. A net like pattern over the flanks distinguishes this goby from others. This appearance comes from the dark outline on the scales.

Life cycle: Has been recorded up to 200 km inland above waterfalls indicating the species may be able to complete its life cycle in fresh water. Little else is known.

Conservation status: Abundant throughout its natural range.

Fishing: Too small to be of interest to anglers except as a bait species.

GOBY, LARGEMOUTH

Scientific name: *Redigobius macrostoma*.
Similar species: Unlikely to be confused with other gobies once mature.

Description: A small goby that has a very compressed body and head. Large males are distinguished by a very large mouth and larger size than females. Snout usually more pointed in females. Colour fades from olive green over the back to a grey white in the belly. Marked with dark blotches, stripes and dots along the dorsal surface and flanks. Few markings on the stomach.

Life cycle: Very little is known, but can be found in fresh water. Most common in estuaries near weed beds.

Conservation status: Abundant throughout its natural range.

Fishing: Can be caught in bait nets and bait traps. Of little use to anglers.

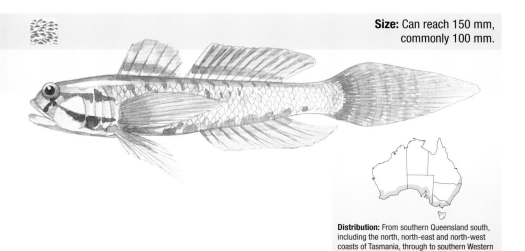

Size: Can reach 150 mm, commonly 100 mm.

Distribution: From southern Queensland south, including the north, north-east and north-west coasts of Tasmania, through to southern Western Australia.

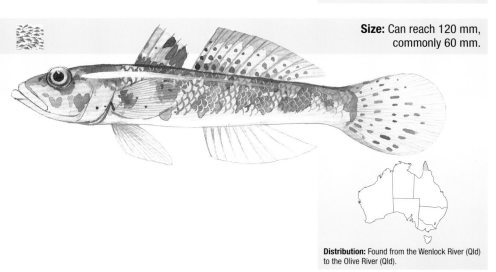

Size: Can reach 120 mm, commonly 60 mm.

Distribution: Found from the Wenlock River (Qld) to the Olive River (Qld).

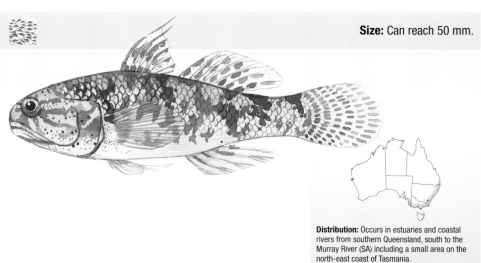

Size: Can reach 50 mm.

Distribution: Occurs in estuaries and coastal rivers from southern Queensland, south to the Murray River (SA) including a small area on the north-east coast of Tasmania.

GOBY, ROMAN NOSE

Scientific name: *Awaos crassilabrus.*
Similar species: Unlikely to be confused with other gobies.

Description: A rounded snout profile is distinctive. Specimens have 8–10 black blotches along the flanks. Eyes prominent on forehead, extending above the head. Can change colour to suit environment, but commonly sandy or light brown.

Life cycle: Little known. Believed to breed in salt water, but has been found as far as 100 km inland in the Pascoe River.

Conservation status: Abundant and common throughout its natural range.

Fishing: Can be eaten, but commonly too small to interest anglers.

GOBY, SPECKLED/BUG EYED

Scientific name: *Redigobius bikolanus.*
Similar species: Largemouth goby *Redigobius macrostoma.*

Description: A very rounded head profile gives the appearance of a short and stout fish. Prominent eyes. Light brown or olive body heavily marked with black or dark brown spots, blotches and speckles. Males are usually larger than females with a bigger head.

Life cycle: Little known, but can complete its entire life cycle in fresh water.

Conservation status: Abundant throughout its natural range.

Fishing: Due to its small size, rarely encountered by anglers.

GOBY, SWAN RIVER

Scientific name: *Pseudogobius olorum.* Also known as Galway's goby, Blue spot goby.
Similar species: Tamar River goby *Afurcagobius tamarensis.*

Description: A small and cylindrical goby with a plump and rounded snout. Males have a slightly larger mouth than females, while females ready to spawn usually have rounded bellies and look swollen. The head and body are light brown fading to a pearly white on the abdomen. Live fish can appear to have gold flecks across the flanks. Dark blotches appear along the flanks with a prominent blotch at the base of the tail.

Life cycle: Little is known, but spawns at the top of estuaries in weed. Spends only part of its life cycle in fresh water.

Conservation status: Common throughout its natural range.

Fishing: Can be collected in shrimp nets, but rarely taken by anglers.

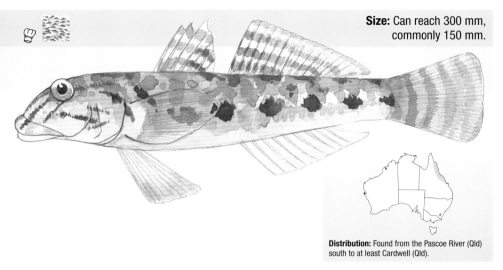

Size: Can reach 300 mm, commonly 150 mm.

Distribution: Found from the Pascoe River (Qld) south to at least Cardwell (Qld).

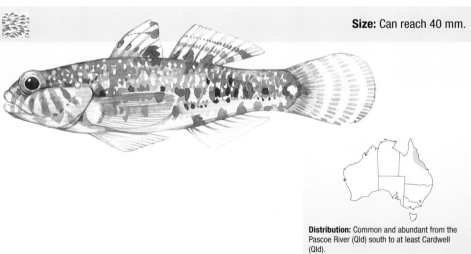

Size: Can reach 40 mm.

Distribution: Common and abundant from the Pascoe River (Qld) south to at least Cardwell (Qld).

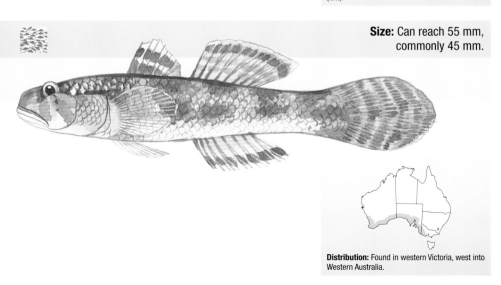

Size: Can reach 55 mm, commonly 45 mm.

Distribution: Found in western Victoria, west into Western Australia.

GOBY, TAMAR RIVER

Scientific name: *Afurcagobius tamarensis.*
Similar species: Swan River goby *Pseudogobius olorum*, Largemouth goby *Redigobius macrostoma*.

Description: Small species with a flattened head and prominent eyes. A large mouth reaching below the eye. Mouth larger in males. Bulbous cheeks and a rounded tail as large as the head. Head and body pale grey on sides and covered with irregular brown markings. In females there is a prominent black spot near the tail, this is absent in mature males. Fins clear or dusky.

Life cycle: Little is known, but prefers sand or silt bottoms in quiet freshwater rivers and estuaries. Believed to breed in spring.

Conservation status: Remains abundant throughout its natural range.

Fishing: Rarely encountered by anglers.

GOBY, TASMANIAN

Scientific name: *Tasmanogobius lordii.*
Similar species: Not likely to be confused with other species.

Description: A very small species that is almost scaleless. Scales appear only in the caudal peduncle and a small patch behind the pectoral fins. Head is small with a bluntly pointed profile. Large mouth. Light brown in colour, 4–6 vertically elongated spots are located along the middle of each flank.

Life cycle: Occurs in streams at the mouths of estuaries, but little else known.

Conservation status: Uncommon.

Fishing: Rarely, if ever, encountered by anglers.

GOLDFISH

Scientific name: *Carassius auratus.* Also known as Golden carp and incorrectly as Crucian carp.
Similar species: Carp *Cyprinus carpio*.

Description: A small, plump fish that is deep bodied and moderately compressed. A large, blunt head with a small mouth and no barbels. Usually olive to deep gold paling on the sides to white on the belly. Rarely bright orange or orange with black marks as in aquarium specimens.

Life cycle: Prefers still and sluggish waters and can survive relatively high water temperatures and poor water quality. May breed more than once in favourable seasons.

Conservation status: An exotic introduced species. Populations are reasonably high and stable where the species exists.

Fishing: Can be caught on light lines and small baits such as worms and glass shrimp. Coarse fishing methods take vast numbers of these fish from many different urban waterways. The species should not be released once caught or used as bait. Dispose of humanely and quickly.

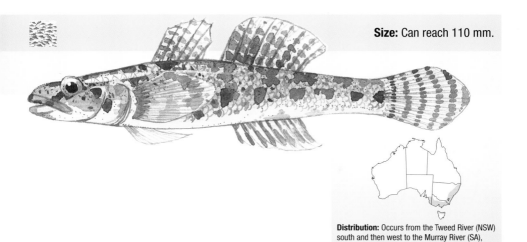

Size: Can reach 110 mm.

Distribution: Occurs from the Tweed River (NSW) south and then west to the Murray River (SA), including the north coast of Tasmania.

Size: Can reach 35 mm, commonly 30 mm.

Distribution: Known only in coastal waters of northern Tasmania.

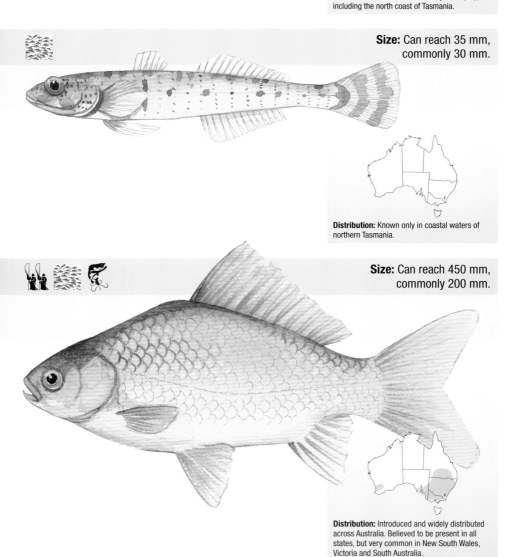

Size: Can reach 450 mm, commonly 200 mm.

Distribution: Introduced and widely distributed across Australia. Believed to be present in all states, but very common in New South Wales, Victoria and South Australia.

GRAYLING, AUSTRALIAN

Scientific name: *Prototroctes maraena*. Also known as Cucumber fish.
Similar species: Yellow-eye mullet *Aldrichetta forsteri*, Freshwater herring *Potamalosa richmondia*.

Description: Slender and compressed with a small head and large eyes. The grayling has a slight smell of cucumbers. A modest forked tail and an adipose fin similar to trout. Colour varies but commonly an olive back fading along the flanks to a silvery white belly. All fin are greyish in colour.

Life cycle: Can live to three years of age, but commonly two. Males mature at age one, females at two years of age. Grayling have a high fecundity with females producing up to 67,000 eggs for a body length of 200 mm. Spawning takes place in fresh water. Juveniles are swept downstream to estuaries and the sea, returning to fresh water during the following spring.

Conservation status: The species is listed as vulnerable by the Australian Society forFish Biology and considered rare in their natural range. They are listed as no take species in Victoria and New South Wales. The population decline has been due to habitat manipulation, expressly the construction of dams and weirs.

Fishing: Listed under the Victorian Flora and Fauna Guarantee Act 1988 and may not be taken.

GRUNTER, BARRED

Scientific name: *Amniataba percoides*. Also known as Stripey grunter.
Similar species: Not likely to be confused with other grunters.

Description: Small mouth and large, prominent eyes. Pointed snout terminates a convex head profile. A small fish that is distinctively coloured. Pale silver colour with five vertical black stripes and whitish or yellow fins. In larger specimens the stripes can pale significantly.

Life cycle: Little is known, but believed to breed from August to March during the wet season. High fecundity with an average 85 g female producing up to 60,000 eggs. Can complete its entire life cycle in fresh water.

Conservation status: Abundant throughout its natural range and where introduced.

Fishing: Too small to be of interest to anglers but is sometimes caught in bait traps intended to catch red claw in Lake Tinaroo.

GRUNTER, COAL

Scientific name: *Hephaestus carbo*. Also known as Golden bream, Chinaman fish.
Similar species: Not likely to be confused with other grunters.

Description: A stout and strong fish with very distinctive gold or yellow blotches and spots along the entire body surface. Has a very sharp opercular spine that should be avoided when handled.

Life cycle: Females have a very high fecundity of small eggs. Spawning may occur in summer or autumn at temperatures exceeding 25ºC.

Conservation status: Abundant throughout its natural range.

Fishing: Can be caught on lure, fly and bait easily. An aggressive species that provides great fun on light tackle. Baits such as shrimp, worms and small terrestrial insect floated across the surface will attract the coal grunter's attention. Small lures and flies that dive or work across the surface are successful.

Eating: Its flesh is considered great table fare.

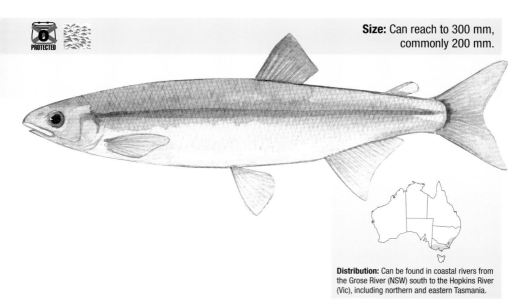

Size: Can reach to 300 mm, commonly 200 mm.

Distribution: Can be found in coastal rivers from the Grose River (NSW) south to the Hopkins River (Vic), including northern and eastern Tasmania.

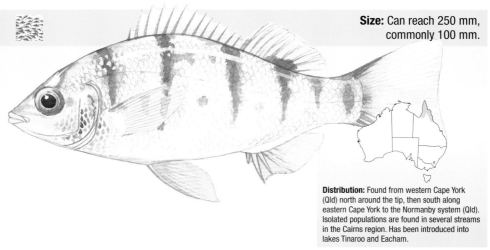

Size: Can reach 250 mm, commonly 100 mm.

Distribution: Found from western Cape York (Qld) north around the tip, then south along eastern Cape York to the Normanby system (Qld). Isolated populations are found in several streams in the Cairns region. Has been introduced into lakes Tinaroo and Eacham.

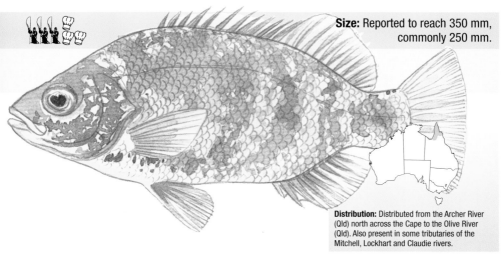

Size: Reported to reach 350 mm, commonly 250 mm.

Distribution: Distributed from the Archer River (Qld) north across the Cape to the Olive River (Qld). Also present in some tributaries of the Mitchell, Lockhart and Claudie rivers.

GRUNTER, GILBERT'S

Scientific name: *Pingalla gilberti*
Similar species: Midgleys grunter *Pingalla midgleyi.*

Description: Small species with a small, downward facing mouth and rounded forehead. Silver to grey in colour with opaque fins.

Life cycle: Little is known, but believed to follow a similar life cycle to other small grunters.

Conservation status: Listed as lower risk-conservation dependent by the Australian Society for Fish Biology.

Fishing: Rarely taken by anglers due to its small size.

GRUNTER, LEATHERY

Scientific name: *Scortum hilli.* Also known as Green-hide jack, Hill's grunter.
Similar species: Barcoo grunter *Scortum barcoo.*

Description: A heavy set body with a rough texture to touch and very firm muscle tone. Small mouth with a prominent black spot near the tail. Colour varies from silver through to a dark browny black depending on environment.

Life cycle: Little is known, but believed to spawn in the early wet season (Oct–Nov). Highly fecund and carries out its entire life cycle in fresh water.

Conservation status: Listed as data deficient by the Australian Society for Fish Biology.

Fishing: Can be caught on lure, fly and bait easily. An aggressive species that provides great fun on light tackle. Baits such as shrimp, worms and small terrestrial insect floated across the surface will attract its attention. Small lures and flies that dive or work across the surface are successful.

Eating: Its flesh is tough and rolls up when cooked. Mostly released upon capture

GRUNTER, LORENTZ'S

Scientific name: *Pingalla lorentzi*
Similar species: Other grunters.

Description: A straight forehead profile with a small mouth and a compressed body that is almost round. Silver in colour, Lorentz's grunters have a distinctive black blotch on the anal fin.

Life cycle: Little is known, but believed to be similar to other freshwater grunters.

Conservation status: Abundant throughout its natural range.

Fishing: Occasionally taken on a baited hook or small lure or fly. Generally too small to be encountered by anglers.

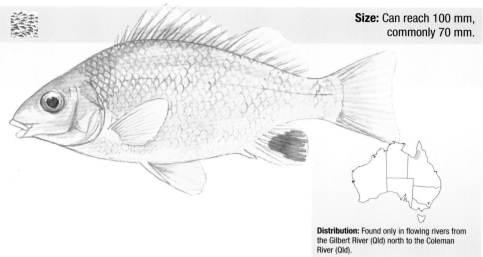

Size: Can reach 100 mm, commonly 70 mm.

Distribution: Found only in flowing rivers from the Gilbert River (Qld) north to the Coleman River (Qld).

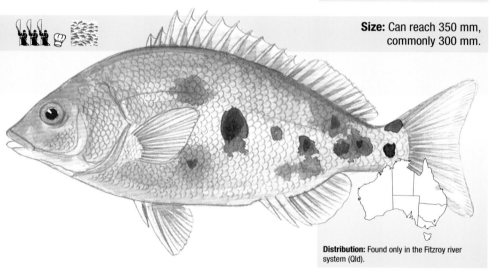

Size: Can reach 350 mm, commonly 300 mm.

Distribution: Found only in the Fitzroy river system (Qld).

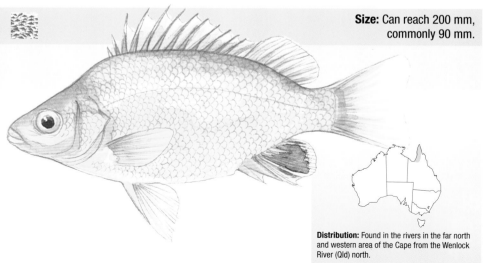

Size: Can reach 200 mm, commonly 90 mm.

Distribution: Found in the rivers in the far north and western area of the Cape from the Wenlock River (Qld) north.

GRUNTER, SOOTY

Scientific name: *Hephaestus fuliginosus*. Also known as Black bream, Sooty.
Similar species: Tully River grunter *Hephaestus* sp.

Description: A strong and robust species that is firm to the touch and heavily scaled. A reasonably large mouth, mid sized eyes and tough, rubbery lips allow this species to eat almost anything. Generally dark to black in colour, occasional individuals can be light brown or show white patches across its body and fins.

Life cycle: Spawning occurs in October and November at selected sites among rocks and rubble. Spawning congregation of between 10 and 200 individual fish congregate at the edge of rapids to spawn in the same area. Spawning activity occurs generally around dusk.

Conservation status: Abundant throughout its natural range.

Fishing: Sooty grunter are easily targeted on lures, flies and baits. They are an extremely aggressive species that can often be observed shouldering each other out of the way to be the first to attack a lure or fly. They are exceptional fighters on all tackle and good angling techniques and tackle are needed to land the majority of fish hooked. Because of its growth potential and fighting ability they have been stocked into many lakes where the species maximum size is being eclipsed every year.

Eating: Sooty grunter have firm and tasty flesh that is excellent eating.

GRUNTER, TULLY RIVER

Scientific name: *Hephaestus* sp.
Similar species: Sooty grunter *Hephaestus fuliginosus*.

Description: A small head and a very tough and firm muscle tone. Very strongly scaled. Usually very dark in colour and may have some lighter flecks across the flanks.

Life cycle: Little is known, but believed to be similar to sooty grunter. Completes its entire life cycle in fresh water.

Conservation status: Common throughout its natural range and where introduced.

Fishing: Can be taken on lure, fly and bait. Small lures should be used if specifically targeting Tully River Grunter. A strong fighter that rates similar to sooty grunter.

Eating: The flesh is firm and provides good eating.

GUDGEON, ARU

Scientific name: *Oxyeleotris aruensis*.
Similar species: Fimbriate gudgeon *Oxyeleotris fimbriatus*.

Description: A small species with a large, rounded tail. Dark brown with lighter, irregular shaped markings on the flanks. Differentiation between the aru and fimbriate gudgeons is in the scale count. Aru gudgeons have a mid-lateral scale count of 55–60, and a transverse scale count of 16–18.

Life cycle: Very little is known.

Conservation status: Widely distributed but never abundant.

Fishing: This species is too small to be of interest to anglers.

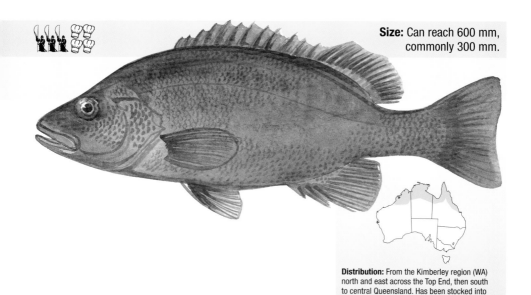

Size: Can reach 600 mm, commonly 300 mm.

Distribution: From the Kimberley region (WA) north and east across the Top End, then south to central Queensland. Has been stocked into several impoundments for recreational fishing.

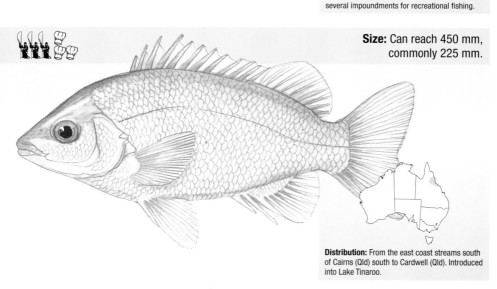

Size: Can reach 450 mm, commonly 225 mm.

Distribution: From the east coast streams south of Cairns (Qld) south to Cardwell (Qld). Introduced into Lake Tinaroo.

Size: Can reach 50 mm, commonly 30 mm.

Distribution: Found in the north of Cape York in the Jardine, Wenlock, Olive and Lockhart/Claudie river drainages (Qld).

GUDGEON, COX'S

Scientific name: *Gobiomorphus coxii*. Also known as Mulgoa gudgeon.
Similar species: Striped gudgeon *Gobiomorphus australis*.

Description: A small and slender species with a rounded head profile. The snout is as broad as it is long. In breeding conditions males are more brightly coloured than females, while females are larger and can have a distended belly. Colour varies from dark brown to olive green with a pale tan belly. A single black or brown stripe down the side is distinctive.

Life cycle: Occurs in flowing waters and rarely found close to the ocean. Has been seen climbing up waterfalls out of the water. Females lay eggs in a nest and males guard this nest. Completes its entire life cycle in fresh water.

Conservation status: Abundant in rivers throughout New South Wales, not so common throughout its Victorian range.

Fishing: Listed under the Flora and Fauna Guarantee Act 1988 and may not be taken.

GUDGEON, CRIMSON-TIPPED

Scientific name: *Butis butis*. Also known as Bony snouted gudgeon.
Similar species: Unlikely to be confused with other gudgeons

Description: A small species with a depressed head and pointed snout. A fairly large mouth and a bony knob at the tip of the snout give this fish a distinctive appearance. Generally blackish brown in colour fading to a lighter brown on the belly. Has a very distinctive black spot on the pectoral fin as well as stripes and blotches across the flanks and cheeks.

Life cycle: Spends the majority of its life in brackish or estuarine water with rare visits into fresh water.

Conservation status: Abundant throughout its natural range.

Fishing: Rarely encountered by anglers.

GUDGEON, DWARF FLATHEAD

Scientific name: *Philypnodon* sp. (undescribed) 1.
Similar species: Flathead gudgeon *Philypnodon grandiceps*.

Description: Similar in appearance to the flathead gudgeon, but smaller. Head broad and flat with a large mouth. Adult males have a much larger mouth than females, a more bulbous head and larger pectoral fins. The head and body are brown to black, covered with irregular blotches. Belly white to grey.

Life cycle: Prefers calm water with a mud and rock bottom with weedy patches. Nothing is known of its breeding.

Conservation status: Common in northern coastal areas, less common in the south and throughout the Murray River.

Fishing: Of little interest to anglers.

PROTECTED

Size: Can reach 190 mm, commonly 150 mm.

Distribution: Occurs in coastal rivers and streams from the Richmond River (NSW) south to Wilsons Promontory (Vic).

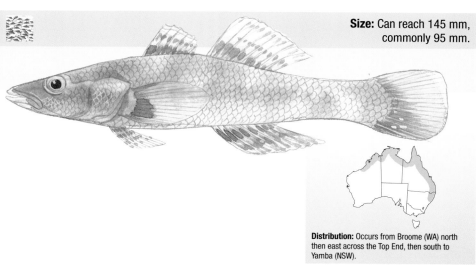

Size: Can reach 145 mm, commonly 95 mm.

Distribution: Occurs from Broome (WA) north then east across the Top End, then south to Yamba (NSW).

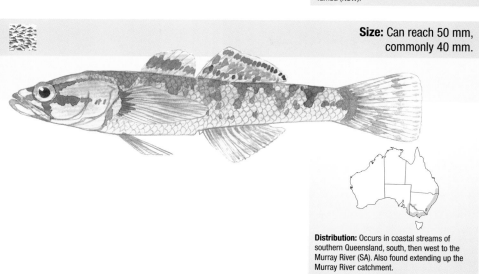

Size: Can reach 50 mm, commonly 40 mm.

Distribution: Occurs in coastal streams of southern Queensland, south, then west to the Murray River (SA). Also found extending up the Murray River catchment.

GUDGEON, FIMBRIATE

Scientific name: *Oxyeleotris fimbriatus.*
Similar species: Aru gudgeon *Oxyeleotris aruensis.*

Description: A small species with a large, rounded tail. Dark brown with lighter, irregular shaped markings on the flanks. Differentiation between the fimbriate and aru gudgeons is in the scale count. Fimbriate gudgeons have a mid-lateral scale count of 60–83, and a transverse scale count of 19–24. Fimbriate gudgeons are also heavier set than aru gudgeons.

Life cycle: Very little is known.

Conservation status: Widely distributed but never abundant.

Fishing: This species is too small to be of interest to anglers.

GUDGEON, FIRETAILED

Scientific name: *Hypseleotris galii.* Also known as Gale's gudgeon.
Similar species: Midgley's carp gudgeon *Hypseleotris* sp. (undescribed), Lake's carp gudgeon *Hypseleotris* sp. (undescribed).

Description: A small species with a very compressed body and head. A small mouth and prominent eye. Breeding males develop a hump on the head behind the eyes and can turn to a dark brown or black colour with intense reddish fins. Males are also larger than females.

Life cycle: Restricted to fresh water where it completes is entire life cycle. Spawning occurs from October to January. Males typically guard eggs.

Conservation status: Remains common throughout its natural range.

Fishing: Rarely encountered by anglers due to its small size.

GUDGEON, FLATHEAD

Scientific name: *Philypnodon grandiceps.* Also known as Big-headed gudgeon, Bullhead, Yarra gudgeon.
Similar species: Dwarf flathead gudgeon *Philypnodon* sp. (undescribed).

Description: Head broad and flat with a large mouth. Adult males have a much larger mouth than females, a more bulbous head and larger pectoral fins. The head and body are brown to black, occasionally reddish brown or yellow and covered with irregular blotches and bands. Belly white to grey, usually with 4–5 dark bands.

Life cycle: Prefers calm water with a mud and rock bottom with weedy patches. Has an extended breeding season in warmer weather. Little else is known.

Conservation status: Common all areas, except less common throughout its Tasmanian range.

Fishing: Of little interest to anglers except as bait where permitted.

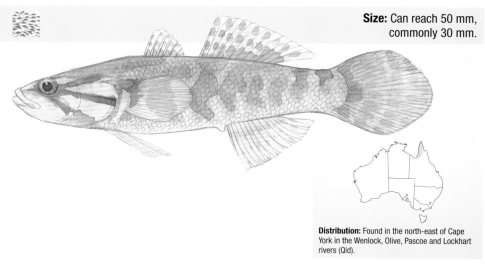

Size: Can reach 50 mm, commonly 30 mm.

Distribution: Found in the north-east of Cape York in the Wenlock, Olive, Pascoe and Lockhart rivers (Qld).

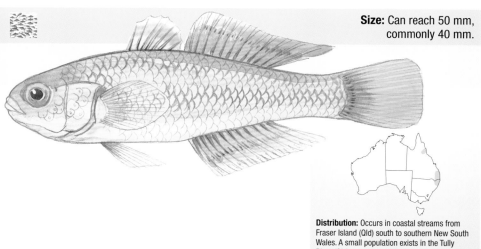

Size: Can reach 50 mm, commonly 40 mm.

Distribution: Occurs in coastal streams from Fraser Island (Qld) south to southern New South Wales. A small population exists in the Tully River (Qld).

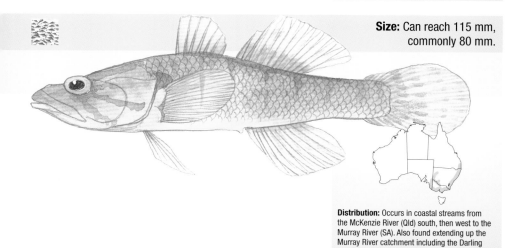

Size: Can reach 115 mm, commonly 80 mm.

Distribution: Occurs in coastal streams from the McKenzie River (Qld) south, then west to the Murray River (SA). Also found extending up the Murray River catchment including the Darling and Murrumbidgee rivers. Occasionally found in northern coastal streams of Tasmania.

GUDGEON, LAKE'S CARP

Scientific name: *Hypseleotris* sp. (undescribed) 2.
Similar species: Midgley's carp gudgeon *Hypseleotris* sp. (undescribed), Firetailed gudgeon *Hypseleotris galii.*

Description: A small fish with a very compressed body and head. Very similar to Midgley's Carp Gudgeon but has a lack of scales on the nape, breast and belly. Males tend to be deeper bodied than females with males developing a hump near the eye and turning darker in colour when ready to breed. Dull brown to purple brown across the entire body. Dorsal and anal fins have distinct white tips and a dusky band below.

Life cycle: Normally found around vegetation. Little else known.

Conservation status: Common throughout its natural range.

Fishing: Rarely encountered by anglers.

GUDGEON, MIDGELEY'S CARP

Scientific name: *Hypseleotris* sp. (undescribed) 3.
Similar species: Lake's carp gudgeon *Hypseleotris* sp. (undescribed), Firetailed gudgeon *Hypseleotris galii.*

Description: A small fish with a very compressed body and head. Very similar to Lake's Carp Gudgeon but has scales on the nape, breast and belly. Males tend to be deeper bodied than females with males developing a hump near the eye and turning darker in colour when ready to breed. Dull brown to purple brown across the entire body. Has vertical reddish stripe across first dorsal fin.

Life cycle: Normally found around vegetation. Little else known.

Conservation status: Common throughout its natural range.

Fishing: Rarely encountered by anglers.

GUDGEON, NORTHERN TROUT

Scientific name: *Mogurnda mogurnda.* Also known as Australian spotted gudgeon, Trout gudgeon.
Similar species: Purple spotted gudgeon *Mogurnda adspersa.*

Description: Very similar to the endangered purple spotted gudgeon, differing in scale count. A slight bulge in the head near the nostrils and a scaleless snout. Dark dorsal surface fading to a patterned green, brown and yellow flank with a white belly. Fins heavily marked and cheeks show radiating dark stripes from the eye.

Life cycle: Breeding believed to be similar to purple spotted gudgeon, but little known. Can survive in bores, muddy dams and rivers.

Conservation status: Common in the northern areas of its range, limited throughout central Australia.

Fishing: Rarely encountered by anglers.

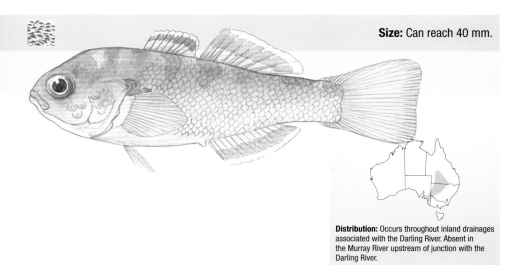

Size: Can reach 40 mm.

Distribution: Occurs throughout inland drainages associated with the Darling River. Absent in the Murray River upstream of junction with the Darling River.

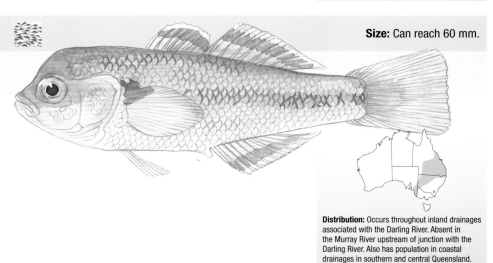

Size: Can reach 60 mm.

Distribution: Occurs throughout inland drainages associated with the Darling River. Absent in the Murray River upstream of junction with the Darling River. Also has population in coastal drainages in southern and central Queensland.

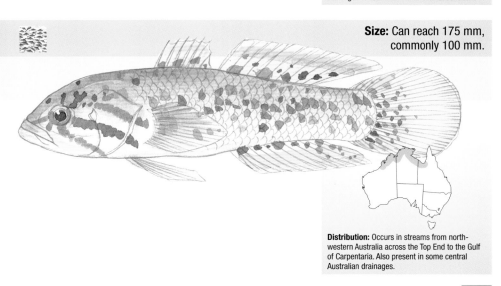

Size: Can reach 175 mm, commonly 100 mm.

Distribution: Occurs in streams from north-western Australia across the Top End to the Gulf of Carpentaria. Also present in some central Australian drainages.

GUDGEON, PORELESS

Scientific name: *Oxyeleotris nullipora.*
Similar species: Unlikely to be confused with other gudgeons.

Description: A small gudgeon with a rounded head profile. Often have a reddish anal fin with broken black dark brown and white blotches across the flanks. In breeding males the belly region can also turn red.

Life cycle: Little known but believed to be able to complete its life cycle in fresh water.

Conservation status: Common throughout its natural range.

Fishing: Too small to be of interest to anglers.

GUDGEON, PURPLE SPOTTED

Scientific name: *Mogurnda adspersa.* Also known as Trout gudgeon, Chequered gudgeon.
Similar species: Northern trout gudgeon *Mogurnda mogurnda.*

Description: A small and robust species with a slightly compressed head and body. Small mouth with males having a hump on the top of the head when ready to breed. Background colour fades from dark chocolate on the dorsal surface to a pale fawn on the ventral surface. Has distinct black blotches along the flanks. Around these patches are many white and red spots often appearing purple with the onset of breeding.

Life cycle: Generally found in slow flowing waters among weeds where suitable hard substrate exists for breeding. Spawns between December and February. Females can spawn repeatedly. Eggs are fanned and protected by males.

Conservation status: Rare, previously believed to be extinct in Victoria. Listed as lower risk conservation dependent by the Australian Society for Fish Biology.

Fishing: Listed under the Victorian Flora and Fauna Guarantee Act 1988 and may not be taken in Victoria.

GUDGEON, SNAKEHEAD

Scientific name: *Ophieleotris aporos.*
Similar species: Unlikely to be confused with other gudgeons.

Description: Large scales and brightly coloured with heavy set bodies. Males tend to be larger and more brightly coloured than females. A large rounded tail and a gently sloping forehead with a prominent eye. Generally black with a cream belly. Males have striking orange and blue markings while females tend to be more golden or yellow.

Life cycle: Spawning takes place on submerged rocks and logs in areas of low flow. It is believed that juveniles need saline water at a certain, undetermined life stage.

Conservation status: Common throughout its natural range.

Fishing: Can be caught on baits intended for other species. Best baits are small shrimp or minnow, fished live on the bottom.

Eating: Not recommended as a food fish due to its average small size. Excellent aquarium fish.

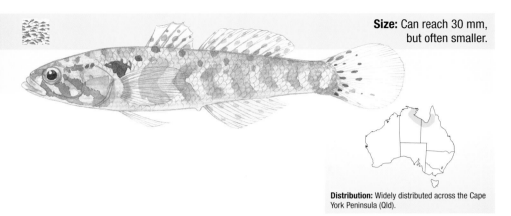

Size: Can reach 30 mm, but often smaller.

Distribution: Widely distributed across the Cape York Peninsula (Qld).

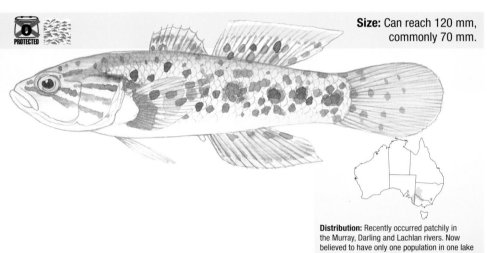

Size: Can reach 120 mm, commonly 70 mm.

Distribution: Recently occurred patchily in the Murray, Darling and Lachlan rivers. Now believed to have only one population in one lake in Victoria. Also exists locally in coastal streams from northern New South Wales to northern Queensland.

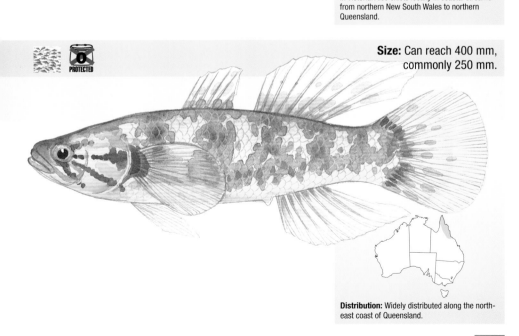

Size: Can reach 400 mm, commonly 250 mm.

Distribution: Widely distributed along the north-east coast of Queensland.

GUDGEON, STRIPED

Scientific name: *Gobiomorphus australis.*
Similar species: Cox's gudgeon *Gobiomorphus coxii.*

Description: A small, stout and robust fish with a head that is more broad than long. Breeding males are much brighter in colour than females displaying an orange anal fin with a lilac fringe. Generally, background colour fades from chocolate brown on the dorsal surface to creamy grey ventrally. Five to seven dark stripes run laterally down the flanks.

Life cycle: Prefers muddy holes in sluggish creeks. Spawns in late summer. Juveniles are washed downstream, migrating back upstream with maturity.

Conservation status: Abundant throughout its natural range.

Fishing: Can be taken in scoop nets aimed at shrimp. A favoured food of Australian bass, this species may make an acceptable live bait where permitted.

GUDGEON, WESTERN CARP

Scientific name: *Hypseleotris klunzingeri.*
Similar species: May be confused with other *Hypseleotris* sp.

Description: A tiny fish with a compressed head and body. Small mouth. Tail less rounded than some other gudgeon species. Males tend to be larger and more slender than females and develop a hump on its head during breeding. Colour is pearly white to yellowish grey, being slightly darker on the dorsal surface. Belly may exhibit some dark blotches.

Life cycle: Lives near vegetation in all habitats with little known about breeding.

Conservation status: Abundant throughout its natural range.

Fishing: Unlikely to be encountered by anglers.

GUPPY

Scientific name: *Poecilia reticulata.*
Similar species: Eastern gambusia *Gambusia holbrooki.*

Description: A small species that can vary markedly in appearance and colouration. Stout and compressed towards the tail, the back arches in front of dorsal fin, especially in females. Small, upturned mouth. Females generally much larger than males but lack the enlarged dorsal fin of males. Females generally drab grey in colour, darker on dorsal surface, fading to silver on the ventral surface. Males highly variable in colour from blue, green, turquoise, red, orange and yellow.

Life cycle: Inhabits only still or gently flowing water where it loosely schools. Does not tolerate water temperatures below 15°C. Breeding is rapid. If males are not present or lacking in numbers in a population, a female can turn into a male.

Conservation status: Introduced exotic species and common where populations have established.

Fishing: Rarely targeted, however may be caught in a dip net. Should not be released back into the wild, as they are an introduced species.

Size: Can reach 175 mm, commonly 120 mm.

Distribution: Occurs in coastal streams from Maryborough (Qld) south to Wilsons Promontory (Vic).

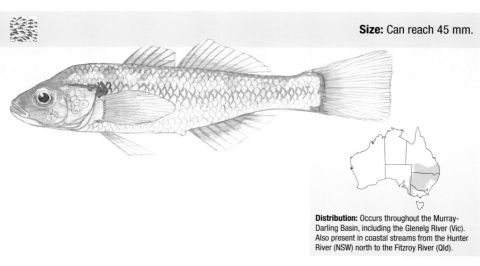

Size: Can reach 45 mm.

Distribution: Occurs throughout the Murray-Darling Basin, including the Glenelg River (Vic). Also present in coastal streams from the Hunter River (NSW) north to the Fitzroy River (Qld).

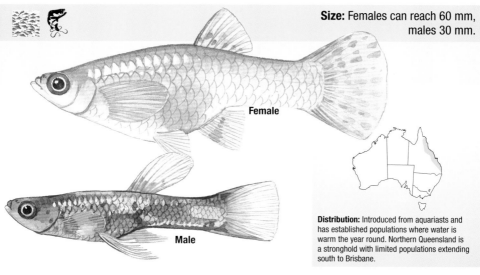

Size: Females can reach 60 mm, males 30 mm.

Female

Male

Distribution: Introduced from aquariasts and has established populations where water is warm the year round. Northern Queensland is a stronghold with limited populations extending south to Brisbane.

HARDYHEAD, DALHOUSIE SPRINGS

Scientific name: *Craterocephalus dahlhousiensis.*
Similar species: Not likely to be confused with other hardyhead because of its limited range.

Description: A deep bodied and robust fish with thick lips and small teeth. This is the only species of hardyhead to display sexual dimorphism with males being slightly smaller than females and with a straighter back. Bright golden on the back with a prominent dark stripe running from the snout, through the eye, to the tail.

Life cycle: Has not been studied in detail. Can tolerate high water temperatures, not low water temperatures. Spawns in June or July.

Conservation status: Abundant in its range, but due to its restricted range is considered vulnerable.

Fishing: Too small to interest anglers.

HARDYHEAD, DARLING RIVER

Scientific name: *Craterocephalus amniculus.*
Similar species: Murray hardyhead *Craterocephalus fluviatilis.*

Description: A small robust fish with thin lips. Two distinct dorsal fins sit atop a slender body. Colour varies with locality but commonly dusky on the dorsal surface fading to a silver on the belly.

Life cycle: Usually found in gently flowing areas near weed beds. Little else known, except that it completes its entire life cycle in fresh water.

Conservation status: Occasionally and patchily abundant. Concern for its status has resulted in it being listed as vulnerable by the Australian Society for Fish Biology.

Fishing: Too small to interest anglers.

HARDYHEAD, FLYSPECKLED

Scientific name: *Craterocephalus stercusmuscarum fulvus.* Also known as Mitchellian hardyhead, Western freshwater hardyhead, Freshwater silverside.
Similar species: Other hardyheads.

Description: A small, slender fish with a downward sloping head. Lips moderately thick with a small mouth. Bright golden yellow to greenish gold on the dorsal surface fading to silver on the belly. A dusky stripe runs from the snout, through the eye, to the tail.

Life cycle: Schools in still or gently flowing water. Spawns from late October through to mid February. Completes entire life cycle in fresh water.

Conservation status: Now rare in southern range, but more common in the northern range and on the east coast of Queensland.

Fishing: Listed under the Victorian Flora and Fauna Guarantee Act 1988 and may not be taken.

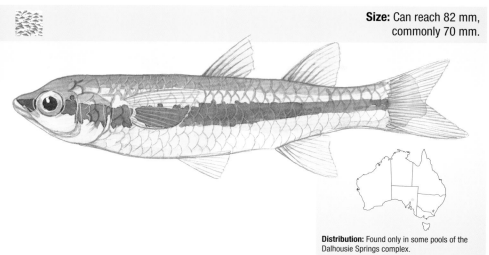

Size: Can reach 82 mm, commonly 70 mm.

Distribution: Found only in some pools of the Dalhousie Springs complex.

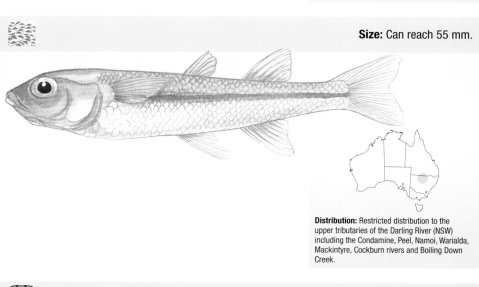

Size: Can reach 55 mm.

Distribution: Restricted distribution to the upper tributaries of the Darling River (NSW) including the Condamine, Peel, Namoi, Warialda, Mackintyre, Cockburn rivers and Boiling Down Creek.

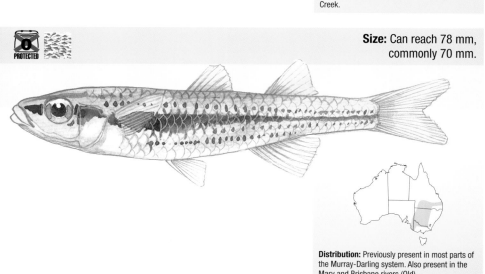

Size: Can reach 78 mm, commonly 70 mm.

Distribution: Previously present in most parts of the Murray-Darling system. Also present in the Mary and Brisbane rivers (Qld).

PROTECTED

HARDYHEAD, GLOVER'S

Scientific name: *Craterocephalus gloveri.*
Similar species: Not likely to be confused with other hardyhead in its natural range.

Description: A slender species with a small mouth. Pale silvery yellow in colour, darker on dorsal surface. Abdomen a pale silvery colour. Has a midlateral stripe running from the snout, through the eye, to the tail.

Life cycle: Restricted to thermal pools at Dalhousie Springs and nothing is known of the breeding of the species.

Conservation status: Is not abundant and isolated populations make this species vulnerable.

Fishing: Too small to be of interest to anglers.

HARDYHEAD, LAKE EYRE

Scientific name: *Craterocephalus eyresii.* Also known as Smelt, Minnow or Whitebait
Similar species: Not likely to be confused with other hardyhead in its natural range.

Description: A robust fish that has increasing body depth with age. Fleshy lips, small mouth. Bright yellow with a distinct silvery midlateral stripe and an iridescent green or silver belly.

Life cycle: Very little is known about the life cycle but appears to be an opportunistic breeder when water levels in Lake Eyre are suitable. Breeds quickly. Able to withstand water salinity three times that of sea water for limited periods.

Conservation status: Population densities are heavily influenced by water levels in Lake Eyre. Individuals maintain the population base in refuge areas during low water levels.

Fishing: Too small to be of interest to anglers.

HARDYHEAD, MARJORIE'S

Scientific name: *Craterocephalus marjoriae.* Also known as Mary River hardyhead.
Similar species: Other hardyheads.

Description: A small and moderately deep bodied species. Head usually blunt and sloping towards the snout. Small mouth. Top of head covered by large, irregularly shaped scales. Body golden to sandy yellow with a dark midlateral stripe. Ventral surface silvery.

Life cycle: Is often found in large schools over a sandy substrate. Indications are that the species spawns in September to October.

Conservation status: Abundant throughout its natural range.

Fishing: Too small to be of interest to anglers, however may be caught in shrimp nets or dip nets and used as a live bait.

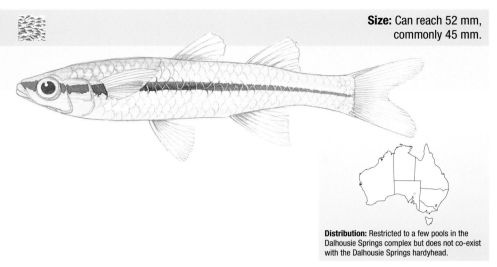

Size: Can reach 52 mm, commonly 45 mm.

Distribution: Restricted to a few pools in the Dalhousie Springs complex but does not co-exist with the Dalhousie Springs hardyhead.

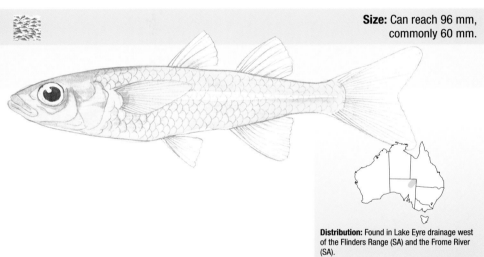

Size: Can reach 96 mm, commonly 60 mm.

Distribution: Found in Lake Eyre drainage west of the Flinders Range (SA) and the Frome River (SA).

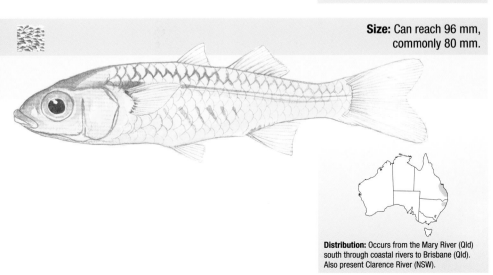

Size: Can reach 96 mm, commonly 80 mm.

Distribution: Occurs from the Mary River (Qld) south through coastal rivers to Brisbane (Qld). Also present Clarence River (NSW).

HARDYHEAD, MURRAY

Scientific name: *Craterocephalus fluviatilis.*
Similar species: Darling River hardyhead *Craterocephalus anniculus.*

Description: A moderately deep bodied species with a small mouth. Scales across the top of the head are irregular in shape. Colour varies from silver to dark golden dorsally, with a silver midlateral stripe. Abdomen is always pale with an iridescent sheen.

Life cycle: Very little is known.

Conservation status: Considered rare and the species is listed as endangered by the Australian Society for Fish Biology.

Fishing: Listed under the Victorian Flora and Fauna Guarantee Act 1988 and may not be taken in Victoria.

HERRING, FRESHWATER

Scientific name: *Potamalosa richmondia.* Also known as Nepean herring.
Similar species: Australian grayling *Prototroctes maraenah.*

Description: Slender and compressed with a long snout and large eye. A small upturned mouth with lower jaw protruding. Strong dorsal fin sits high on the back. Tail strongly forked. Bright silvery with a somewhat iridescent back. Can occasionally have stripes along the back or flanks.

Life cycle: Prefers clear, moderate flowing streams and rivers. Very little is known of its spawning, but believed to require saltwater to complete its life cycle.

Conservation status: Not considered under threat, but numbers fluctuate and the species is not common.

Fishing: Can be caught on small dry flies by specifically targeting riffles and runs in larger rivers on the New South Wales north coast. Listed under the Victorian Flora and Fauna Guarantee Act 1988 and may not be taken in Victoria.

HERRING, OX-EYE

Scientific name: *Megalops cyprinoides.* Also known as Tarpon.
Similar species: Should not be confused with any other species.

Description: A compressed fish with a very large eye and upward turned mouth. Thick scales and a heavily forked tail. Easily identified by the trailing filament on the dorsal fin. Silver in colour, darker on the dorsal surface and occasionally metallic in appearance on the belly.

Life cycle: The ox-eye herring is essentially a marine species. Spawning occurs in the summer months and is believed to take place in estuaries and shallow bays. The eggs are pelagic. Juveniles move into the fresh water. Specimens in the fresh can reach 400 mm on average, very occasionally reaching 600 mm.

Conservation status: Abundant throughout its natural range.

Fishing: Ox-eye herring are greatly valued as a sportfishing target. They eagerly take lures and flies, being more selective and finicky towards live and dead baits. Its large eye is a great tool for hunting and the species uses this to the utmost advantage when feeding. Anglers working a lure or fly close to a school of ox-eye herring are usually rewarded with a positive strike. A solid hook-up is harder to achieve as its mouth is verybony.

Eating: Ox-eye herring have many bones and its flesh is soft and tasteless. Most are released unharmed.

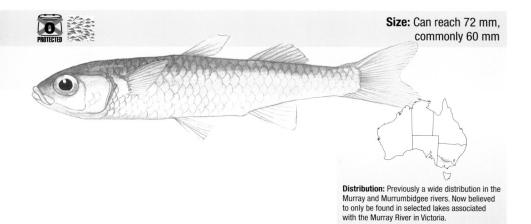

Size: Can reach 72 mm, commonly 60 mm

Distribution: Previously a wide distribution in the Murray and Murrumbidgee rivers. Now believed to only be found in selected lakes associated with the Murray River in Victoria.

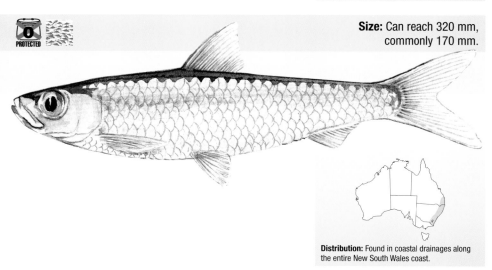

Size: Can reach 320 mm, commonly 170 mm.

Distribution: Found in coastal drainages along the entire New South Wales coast.

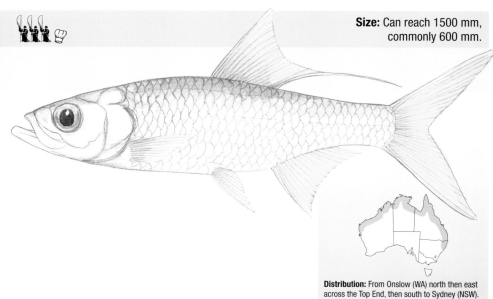

Size: Can reach 1500 mm, commonly 600 mm.

Distribution: From Onslow (WA) north then east across the Top End, then south to Sydney (NSW).

JOLLYTAIL, COMMON

Scientific name: *Galaxias maculatus*. Also known as Common galaxias.
Similar species: Murray jollytail *Galaxias rostratus*.

Description: A slender and streamlined fish with a small, blunt head and large eyes. Small mouth and thin fins. Translucent grey-olive with irregular greenish blotches. Belly bright silver and without markings.

Life cycle: Can tolerate a wide variety of habitats. Most commonly found in lakes and slow flowing rivers. Adults migrate downstream to spawn, laying eggs on submerged terrestrial vegetation. The eggs can be left high and dry for up to two weeks until spring tides cover them again. They young then hatch and swim to sea, migrating back to the rivers after six months.

Conservation status: Widely abundant throughout its range.

Fishing: Forms an important part of the Tasmanian whitebait fishery and is widely used as bait in many lakes and rivers throughout Australia. Can be collected in bait traps, dip nets or whitebait nets where allowed.

JOLLYTAIL, MURRAY

Scientific name: *Galaxias rostratus*. Also known as Flatheaded galaxias.
Similar species: Common jollytail *Galaxias maculatus*.

Description: Similar to the common jollytail but has a slightly more flattened head and a larger mouth. Olive green on the back and sides with irregular dark green or grey blotches along the flanks. Bright silver below the lateral line.

Life cycle: Found mostly in gentle flowing areas of the rivers including off-river lagoons in shoals. Breeds when water temperature is cool between 9–14ºC.

Conservation status: Intermittent populations that rarely intermingle has seen this species listed as vulnerable.

Fishing: Of little interest to anglers.

LAMPREY, NON-PARASITIC

Scientific name: *Mordacia praecox*.
Similar species: Pouched lamprey *Geotria australis*, Small headed lamprey *Mordacia mordax*.

Description: Long and cylindrical with distinct gill openings. Ammocoete brown and darker on the dorsal surface. Bluish black on the dorsal surface once mature. Ventral surface yellowish in females and grey in males.

Life cycle: Ammocoetes metamorphose at lengths between 130 and 170 mm. Enters metamorphose in late spring, spawning the following winter. The non-parasitic lamprey does not feed once mature.

Conservation status: Listed as vulnerable, but difficult to determine population numbers because of identification problems.

Fishing: Rarely encountered by anglers as the ammocoete filter feeds and the adult does not feed.

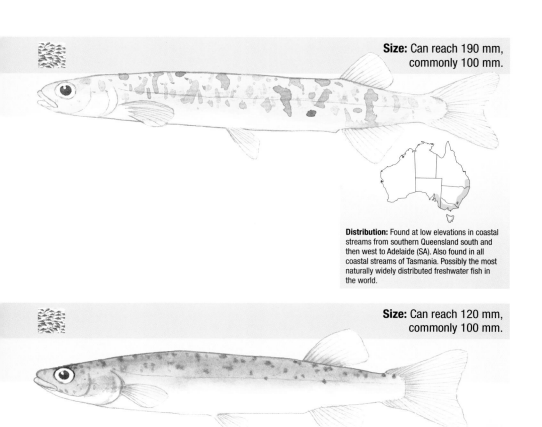

Size: Can reach 190 mm, commonly 100 mm.

Distribution: Found at low elevations in coastal streams from southern Queensland south and then west to Adelaide (SA). Also found in all coastal streams of Tasmania. Possibly the most naturally widely distributed freshwater fish in the world.

Size: Can reach 120 mm, commonly 100 mm.

Distribution: Known only in the Murray-Darling system, especially low elevation areas.

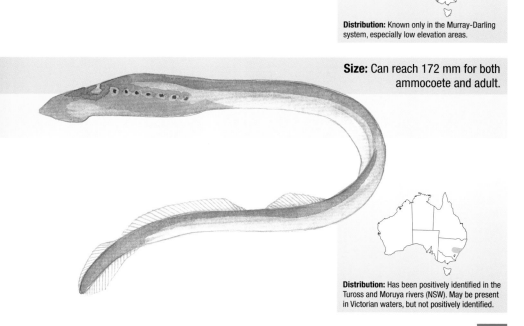

Size: Can reach 172 mm for both ammocoete and adult.

Distribution: Has been positively identified in the Tuross and Moruya rivers (NSW). May be present in Victorian waters, but not positively identified.

LAMPREY, POUCHED

Scientific name: *Geotria australis.*
Similar species: Short headed lamprey *Mordacia mordax,* Non-Parasitic lamprey *Mordacia praecox.*

Description: Ammocoete typically light brown with a slightly darker dorsal surface. Young adults are silver with bright blue bands along back that persist throughout sea life and early return to fresh water. Becomes increasingly drab the longer the time spent in fresh water.

Life cycle: Ammocoete enters metamorphosis at age 4½. Young adults migrate to sea and attach to a host species. Host species are commonly bream, salmon, tailor and occasionally barracouta. Adults return in winter on its spawning run. Spawning run may last for up to 16 months.

Conservation status: Still abundant but believed to be in decline due to habitat manipulation.

Fishing: Rarely encountered by anglers in Australia. Maori people in New Zealand trap and net the species as a food fish.

LAMPREY, SHORT HEADED

Scientific name: *Mordacia mordax.*
Similar species: Non-Parasitic lamprey *Mordacia praecox*, Pouched lamprey *Geotria australis.*

Description: Ammocoete eyeless and overall brownish in colour. Adults have a well developed suctorial disc with radially arranged teeth. Once sexually mature, the adults lose the radial tooth plates. Adults are initially bluish grey and silver ventrally, becoming duller and greyer during the spawning run.

Life cycle: Metamorphosis starts at age three and takes six months on average. Young adults feed in estuaries by attaching to a host fish such as bream and mullet. They also feed on barracouta once migration has reached the sea. The spawn run starts in late winter and can last a year.

Conservation status: Abundant throughout its natural range.

Fishing: Rarely encountered by anglers, except when attached to a host fish.

Size: Ammocoete can reach 120 mm,
Adult can reach 700 mm, commonly 500 mm.

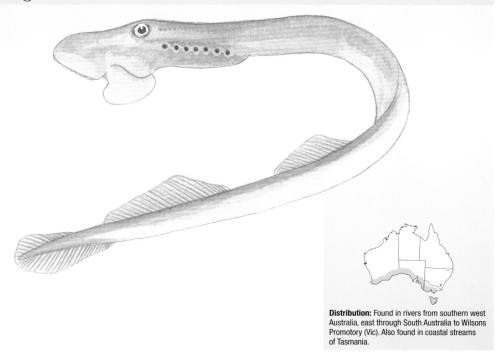

Distribution: Found in rivers from southern west Australia, east through South Australia to Wilsons Promotory (Vic). Also found in coastal streams of Tasmania.

Size: Ammocoete can reach 140 mm,
Adult can reach 440 mm, commonly 300 mm.

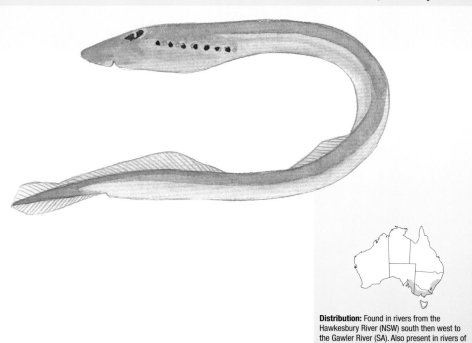

Distribution: Found in rivers from the Hawkesbury River (NSW) south then west to the Gawler River (SA). Also present in rivers of Tasmania.

LONG TOM, FRESHWATER

Scientific name: *Strongylura kreffti*. Also known as Needle fish, Alligator gar.
Similar species: There are several similar marine species of long tom that do not enter freshwater.

Description: Easily identified by having both jaws extended and full of needle sharp teeth. A large eye and a tough, bony head. Body is long and slender and may have black spots along the flanks. Usually silver in colour, some individuals can have a darkened dorsal surface.

Life cycle: Long Tom spawn in fresh water attaching eggs to weeds and reeds. Juveniles are common prior to flooding, which may be of aid in distributing the species throughout a waterway.

Conservation status: Abundant throughout its natural range.

Fishing: Can be targeted on lures, flies and baits. Its hard, bony mouth make this species difficult to hook, but once hooked they leap and gyrate for the entire fight. Care needs to be taken when unhooking the fish as they can bite the hand that releases them, causing damage.

Eating: Long Tom are not considered a great delicacy as they are slender and bony.

LUNGFISH, AUSTRALIAN

Scientific name: *Neoceratodus forsteri*. Also known as Queensland lungfish.
Similar species: Unlike any other species.

Description: The most primitive of Australian fish, the lungfish is a large scaled species with a small eye and a large head. Colour varies from dark chocolate brown to light brown, lightening towards the belly and sometimes appearing yellow. Large pectoral fins sit low on the body, while the pelvic fins are set well back towards the thick, eel-like tail.

Life cycle: Spawning takes place over shallow weed in fresh water where the male and female complete a complex courtship ritual. Eggs are deposited in weed near the water's edge. Lungfish complete its entire life cycle in fresh water. One of the few fish species that can actually breath air at the surface of the water.

Conservation status: Extremely rare, the lungfish has been introduced into selected waterways to build numbers of individuals.

Fishing: Lungfish are a totally protected species and may not be specifically targeted by anglers.

Distribution: Widely distributed from northern New South Wales, north and then west across the Top End to Carnarvon (WA).

PROTECTED

Size: Can reach 1500 mm.

Distribution: Naturally found only in the Mary and Burnett rivers (Qld), the species has been introduced into the Brisbane, Albert and Coomera rivers as well as Enoggerra Reservoir (Qld).

MANGROVE JACK

Scientific name: *Lutjanus argentimaculatus.* Also known as Red devil, Red fish, Red bream.
Similar species: Red bass *Lutjanus bohar.*

Description: Mangrove jack are a powerfully built fish with a mid sized mouth filled with conical canine-like teeth. Large eyes, sharp operculum and stout spines make this fish a real handful when landed. A red coloration across the entire body when mature, juveniles can exhibit a set of vertical white bars down the flanks.

Life cycle: Spawning occurs in estuaries and along coastal flats as adults move to offshore reefs. Can be bred in captivity under strictly controlled conditions. Little else is commonly known.

Conservation status: Abundant throughout its natural range.

Fishing: Mangrove jack are much sought after by sport anglers chasing a quick thrill. A habit of mangrove jack is to come out of its hole and attack a lure, fly or bait as it speeds back towards its hole. This attack and feeding style sees anglers getting very passionate and frustrated with the species. Quality tackle, tight drag settings and good technique are needed to land more jacks than you lose.

Eating: Mangrove jack make excellent eating with firm, white flesh.

MILKFISH

Scientific name: *Chanos chanos.*
Similar species: Giant herring *Elops machnata.*

Description: A small toothless mouth indicates this species is a vegetarian. It has a large eye and a large deeply forked tail that provides enormous power. A brilliant silver colour that can be slightly darker on the dorsal surface.

Life cycle: Fecundity is high with as many as six million eggs being laid by a large female. Spawning is believed to occur on moonless nights over sandy areas. Little else is known.

Conservation status: Common throughout its natural range.

Fishing: Milkfish are an important commercial aquaculture species in many parts of the world. Juveniles are collected in nets from sandy bays. Anglers chase milkfish with fly tackle and enjoy a great fight. They are a fast and powerful fish that takes long runs and does not give up. Bread imitation flies fished in berley trails are the most successful way of fishing. Can sometimes be caught by bait anglers fishing pipi or prawn pieces on light tackle. Rarely are these fish landed on light tackle.

Eating: Considered poor table fare in Australia, but a delicacy in Indonesia.

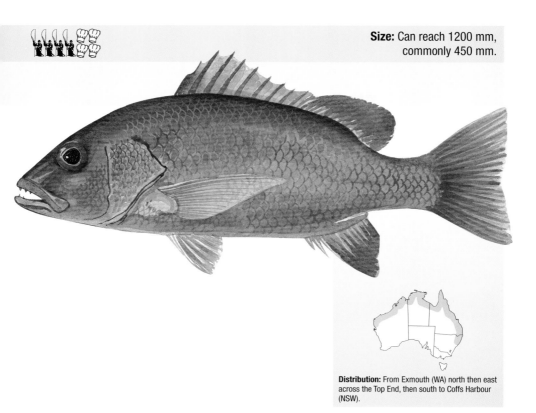

Distribution: From Exmouth (WA) north then east across the Top End, then south to Coffs Harbour (NSW).

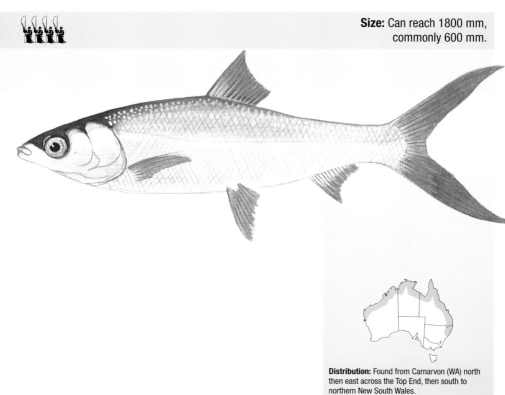

Distribution: Found from Carnarvon (WA) north then east across the Top End, then south to northern New South Wales.

MOLLY, SAILFIN

Scientific name: *Poecilia latipinna.*
Similar species: Guppy *Poecilia reticulata.*

Description: Deep bodied and highly compressed with a small mouth and large eye. Dorsal fin large in males and small in females. Olive on back, paling to an iridescent violet on the sides with orange spots. Belly silvery white with a bluish sheen. Dorsal fin strongly coloured olive and rimmed with orange in male, more pale in females.

Life cycle: Can tolerate salinities to as great as sea water, preferring still or gently flowing water. Ovoviviparous, producing live young, approximately 120 young per brood.

Conservation status: Introduced exotic species.

Fishing: Too small to be of interest to anglers, however can be collected by using a dip net. Specimens should not be returned to the water.

MOUTH ALMIGHTY

Scientific name: *Glossamia aprion.* Also known as Northern mouth-breeder, Queensland mouth-brooder, Gills cardinalfish, Flabby, Stinker.
Similar species: Unlikely to be confused with other species.

Description: As the name implies, this species has a large mouth that is slightly upturned. A large eye with a darker band extending through it from the snout to the shoulder region. Generally brown in colour, this may vary with environment. Flanks are covered with blotches and irregular markings.

Life cycle: Mouth almighty are believed to breed all year round when water temperatures are at or above 22ºC. The male broods the eggs in the mouth for two weeks and the young leave the mouth once the egg sac is absorbed.

Conservation status: Common throughout its natural range.

Fishing: Mouth almighty can be taken on small lures aimed at archer fish or similar small species. Its large mouth and aggressive nature far outshine its fight on rod and reel. Can also be caught as a by-catch in nets set for redclaw in Lake Tinaroo.

Eating: Larger specimens are believed to be good eating, but its average small size sees the fish being used more for bait than for food.

MOUTHBROODER, MOZAMBIQUE

Scientific name: *Oreochromis mossambicus.* Also known as Mozambique cichlid.
Similar species: Black mangrove cichlid *Tilapia mariae.*

Description: Medium sized and deep, compressed body. Small mouth with rubbery lips and a large eye. In males the jaws can become enlarged to give a slight concave profile to the head. Colour varies from dark grey/green on the dorsal surface to pale olive on the flanks.

Life cycle: Males excavate a basin shaped pit in amongst shallow weed where the females lay their eggs. The males releases milt over the eggs and the females takes up the egg and milt into her mouth. Fry hatch after 3–5 days and are released from the mouth after 14 days. Young fish stay close to the female, darting into her mouth when danger approaches.

Conservation status: Common throughout its range.

Fishing: Has little angler value and is regarded as a pest species.

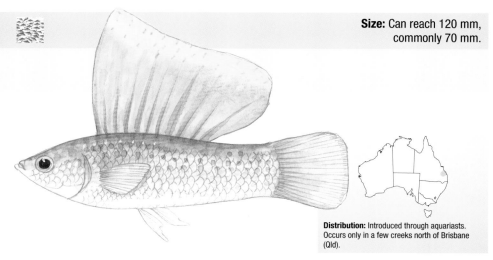

Size: Can reach 120 mm, commonly 70 mm.

Distribution: Introduced through aquariasts. Occurs only in a few creeks north of Brisbane (Qld).

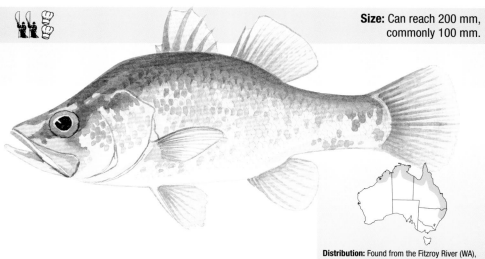

Size: Can reach 200 mm, commonly 100 mm.

Distribution: Found from the Fitzroy River (WA), north and then east across the Top End and Cape York, then south to Coffs Harbour (NSW).

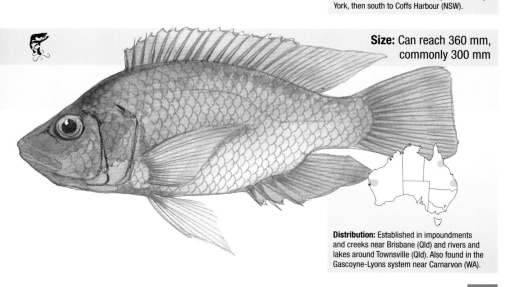

Size: Can reach 360 mm, commonly 300 mm

Distribution: Established in impoundments and creeks near Brisbane (Qld) and rivers and lakes around Townsville (Qld). Also found in the Gascoyne-Lyons system near Carnarvon (WA).

MUDFISH, TASMANIAN

Scientific name: *Galaxias cleaveri*. Also known as Mud trout, Mud galaxias.
Similar species: Common jollytail *Galaxias maculatus*, Swamp galaxias *Galaxias parvus*.

Description: An elongate and tubular species with a short and blunt head. Very small eyes and distinctive nostril above lip. Greenish brown on back and sides, fading to a greyish white on the belly. Marked with irregular dark stripes and blotches across the flanks and fins.

Life cycle: Found in still, heavily vegetated water. Has the ability to aestivate, which is to survive under logs, rocks and other structure, when free water dries up. Spawning occurs in winter and the newly hatched larvae swim to sea for 2–3 months, returning as a minor part of the whitebait runs in Tasmania. Diet is little studied.

Conservation status: Abundant and common throughout its natural range.

Fishing: May be caught in whitebait nets in Tasmania. In Victoria the species is protected and may not be caught or used as bait.

MULLET, FRESHWATER

Scientific name: *Myxis petardi*. Also known as Pinkeye mullet.
Similar species: Sea mullet *Mugil cephalus*.

Description: A stout fish that is small to moderate in size. Small, pointed head and large eye. Dark olive on the back, silver on sides and silver or white on the ventral surface.

Life cycle: Generally found in slow moving pools in small shoals. Reaches maturity at four years of age. Highly fecund with females laying between 1–3 million eggs. Most spawning occurs in February.

Conservation status: Abundant throughout its natural range.

Fishing: Can be caught on small hooks, fished under floats, baited with dough or worm.

Eating: The flesh is palatable but can have a muddy flavour when taken from slow flowing and muddy rivers.

MULLET, SEA

Scientific name: *Mugil cephalus*. Also known as Bully mullet, River mullet.
Similar species: All other mullets.

Description: A thickly muscled species that is quite cylindrical in shape. A broad, flat head and large eye with a moderately forked tail. Large scales and a gelatinous film covering the body and head. Generally green or olive over the dorsal surface, silver on the flanks and silvery white on the belly.

Life cycle: Can spend several years in fresh water, but a freshwater life stage is not necessary. Breeding is believed to take place in the ocean. Juveniles have been recorded in freshwater rivers. Feeds mainly on detritus, algae and diatoms.

Conservation status: Abundant throughout its natural range.

Fishing: Can be taken on baits such as bread, worm and peeled prawn fished on small hooks under floats. Difficult to catch, but an exceptional fighting fish on any line.

Eating: The flesh is good to eat, although those caught in fresh water can taste a little weedy or muddy.

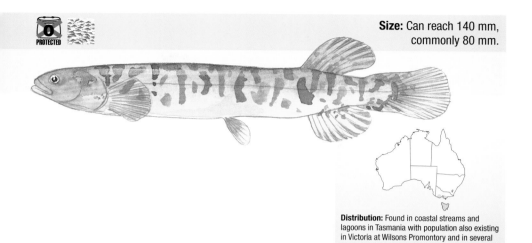

Distribution: Found in coastal streams and lagoons in Tasmania with population also existing in Victoria at Wilsons Promontory and in several Otway Ranges rivers.

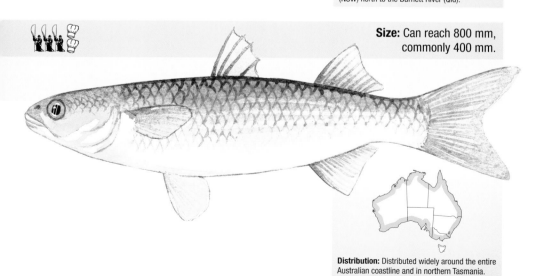

Size: Can reach 800 mm, commonly 300 mm.

Distribution: Found from the Georges River (NSW) north to the Burnett River (Qld).

Size: Can reach 800 mm, commonly 400 mm.

Distribution: Distributed widely around the entire Australian coastline and in northern Tasmania. Strong populations exist in southern Queensland and northern New South Wales.

MULLET, YELLOW-EYE

Scientific name: *Aldrichetta forsteri*. Also known as Sea mullet.
Similar species: Other mullets when small.

Description: Distinctive and moderate sized yellow rimmed eyes are distinguishing. A slender and elongate body that is olive green on the back, silver on the sides and white on the belly.

Life cycle: Spends the majority of its life in the sea or estuaries, but can be found in fresh water throughout the year and throughout its entire range. Spawns in the sea and juveniles move into the estuaries to grow and mature. Feeds mainly on detritus, but also takes small animals such as shrimp, crabs and occasionally small fish.

Conservation status: Abundant throughout its natural range.

Fishing: Readily taken on soft baits such as bread, pipi or marine worms. Can occasionally be taken on whitebait, bluebait and cut pilchard. A good fighter that is a common capture for children on piers and jetties.

Eating: The flesh is tasty and firm, but fish should be cleaned immediately upon capture.

PARAGALAXIAS, ARTHURS

Scientific name: *Paragalaxias mesotes*.
Similar species: Western paragalaxias *Paragalaxias julianus*, Shannon paragalaxias *Paragalaxias dissimilis*, Great Lake paragalaxias *Paragalaxias eleotroides*.

Description: A small, stout and bullet shaped species with a sloping and blunt head. Large mouth with equal length jaws. Small dorsal fin. A boldly coloured fish that is dark green on the back, fragmenting on the sides into isolated patches and bands. Paler colouration on the trunk and belly silvery grey.

Life cycle: Found in still water amongst rocks and vegetation. Very little is known about the life cycle although it is entirely completed in fresh water.

Conservation status: Listed as vulnerable by the Australian Society for Fish Biology, this species has never been found in large numbers.

Fishing: Not recommended as a target species.

PARAGALAXIAS, GREAT LAKE

Scientific name: *Paragalaxias eleotroides*. Also known as Great Lake galaxias.
Similar species: Arthurs paragalaxias *Paragalaxias mesotes*, Shannon paragalaxias *Paragalaxias dissimilis*, Western paragalaxias *Paragalaxias julianus*.

Description: A small, stout species that is flattened on the ventral surface. Moderate sized mouth with equal length jaws and located low on the head. Prominent dorsal fin. Light brownish to gold fading to a silvery green on the belly. No distinctive stripes, but irregular blotching.

Life cycle: Found amongst cover and under rocks and entire life cycle is completed in fresh water. Little is known of the breeding habits, but believed to breed in October and November.

Conservation status: Not common, but listed as vulnerable by the Australian Society for Fish Biology due to sharing its habitat with brown and rainbow trout.

Fishing: Not recommended as a target species.

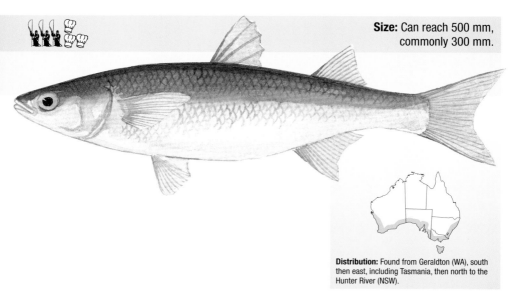

Size: Can reach 500 mm, commonly 300 mm.

Distribution: Found from Geraldton (WA), south then east, including Tasmania, then north to the Hunter River (NSW).

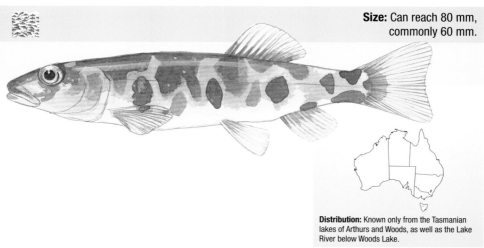

Size: Can reach 80 mm, commonly 60 mm.

Distribution: Known only from the Tasmanian lakes of Arthurs and Woods, as well as the Lake River below Woods Lake.

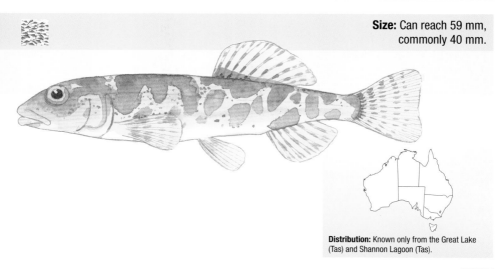

Size: Can reach 59 mm, commonly 40 mm.

Distribution: Known only from the Great Lake (Tas) and Shannon Lagoon (Tas).

PARAGALAXIAS, SHANNON

Scientific name: *Paragalaxias dissimilis.* Also known as Shannon galaxias.
Similar species: Arthurs paragalaxias *Paragalaxias mesotes,* Great Lake paragalaxias *Paragalaxias eleotroides,* Western paragalaxias *Paragalaxias julianus.*

Description: A small bullet shaped fish with a long, flattened snout. Large mouth with equal length jaws. A long and rounded dorsal fin is distinctive. Olive brown to grey green on the dorsal surface that can appear gold in certain light. Indistinct dark blotches cover the sides.

Life cycle: Found among cover and rocks during the day, but believed to swim freely mid-water during the night to feed. Spawning occurs from December to January with fecundity low at 40–180 eggs per female. Both sexes are mature after one year and individuals can live for three years.

Conservation status: The species is listed as vulnerable by the Australian Society for Fish Biology.

Fishing: Rarely encountered by anglers.

PARAGALAXIAS, WESTERN

Scientific name: *Paragalaxias julianus.*
Similar species: Arthurs paragalaxias *Paragalaxias mesotes,* Shannon paragalaxias *Paragalaxias dissimilis,* Great Lake paragalaxias *Paragalaxias eleotroides.*

Description: A stout species that is bullet shaped and tapering to a slender tail. A long, flattened head with a blunt snout.

Life cycle: Found among rocks, especially where they are spaced apart. Little is known of reproduction, but life cycle is completed entirely in fresh water.

Conservation status: Abundant throughout its natural habitat.

Fishing: Of little interest to anglers.

PENNY FISH

Scientific name: *Denariusa bandata.*
Similar species: Macleay's perchlet *Ambassis macleayi,* Agassiz's glassfish *Ambassis agassizi.*

Description: An ovate fish with a large eye and small mouth. Light olive in colour with a silvery abdomen, there are 5–6 dark stripes running vertically along the flanks. A bright blue spot is situated on the operculum and a small dark spot is situated at the base of the pectoral fin.

Life cycle: Little is known, but appear to prefer lagoons and slow flowing areas in rivers where weed has established.

Conservation status: Common throughout its natural range.

Fishing: Of little interest to anglers, but occasionally used as bait.

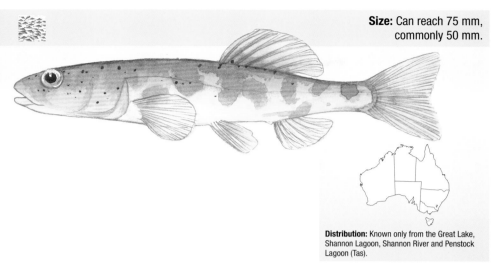

Size: Can reach 75 mm, commonly 50 mm.

Distribution: Known only from the Great Lake, Shannon Lagoon, Shannon River and Penstock Lagoon (Tas).

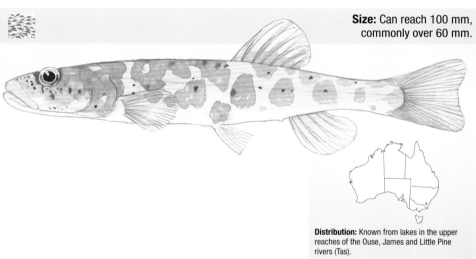

Size: Can reach 100 mm, commonly over 60 mm.

Distribution: Known from lakes in the upper reaches of the Ouse, James and Little Pine rivers (Tas).

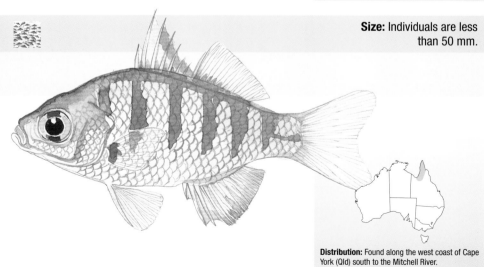

Size: Individuals are less than 50 mm.

Distribution: Found along the west coast of Cape York (Qld) south to the Mitchell River.

PERCH, ESTUARY

Scientific name: *Macquaria colonorum.*
Similar species: Australian bass *Macquaria novemaculeata.*

Description: A moderate sized fish with an ovate and laterally compressed body. Adults have a snout tapered inwardly (concave) with a large eye. Pelvic fins are a uniform grey colour. Most other features similar to that of the Australian bass. Colour varies from dark grey and silver on the dorsal surface to metallic silver on the flanks and almost white on the belly.

Life cycle: Lives in tidal waters and requires saltwater to breed. Commonly found in fresh water throughout their range. Males reach maturity at 220 mm, females at 280 mm. Highly fecund with planktonic and transparent eggs. Breeds in winter when water temperatures are 14°–19°C depending on the population's location.

Conservation status: Difficult to assess but believed to be common throughout its natural range.

Fishing: Readily taken on bait, lure and fly, the estuary perch is becoming recognised as a quality sport fishing species. Casting lures, flies and baits into snags and boulder areas in freshwater rivers that access the sea will bring the best results. Shrimps or worms are the best baits, while small lures and flies in the 3–6 cm range are ideal. Fishing during the low light periods of dawn and dusk are most productive, however good catches can be taken during the night or during the day.

Eating: The flesh is moist and excellent eating.

PERCH, EWEN PYGMY

Scientific name: *Nannoperca variegata.* Also known as Variegated pygmy perch.
Similar species: Southern pygmy perch *Nannoperca australis*, Oxeleyan pygmy perch *Nannoperca oxleyana.*

Description: Moderately compressed body with a small mouth. Moderate eye. Colour variable, but commonly creamish white to green dorsally, changing to orange below. Usually has a dark spot near the base of the caudal fin. Can have dark blotches mid laterally.

Life cycle: Associated with dense vegetation with high water flow. May live for 3–4 years and is a protracted breeder. High fecundity for the species with the ability to produce 5,000 ova at varying stages of maturity.

Conservation status: Locally abundant where found, but the limited geographical distribution means populations can quickly come under threat and is listed as vulnerable by the Australian Society for Fish Biology.

Fishing: Of little interest to anglers.

Distribution: Found in coastal lakes and rivers from the Richmond River (NSW) south then west through Victoria to the Murray River (SA). A population also exists in the Arthur and Ansons rivers (Tas).

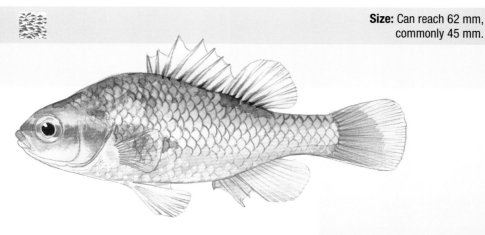

Distribution: Known only from Ewen Ponds (SA) and in some tributaries of the Glenelg River (Vic).

PERCH, GOLDEN

Scientific name: *Macquaria ambigua.* Also known as Yellowbelly, Callop, Murray perch.
Similar species: Macquarie perch *Macquaria australasica*.

Description: A moderate to large species that is oval and laterally compressed. Moderate sized eyes and mouth with a distinct humping of the shoulders on larger specimens. Head profile below the hump appears concave. Colour varies from olive green to a milky white depending on habitat and water conditions. Clear water fish can be spectacular with dark shoulders and flanks changing to bright yellow bellies and fins.

Life cycle: Golden perch are a highly mobile species moving about when water levels rise, or during the spawning season. Highly fecund, a 2.5 kg female is capable of producing 500,000 eggs. Spawning takes place in spring when water temperatures rise above 22ºC. Eggs are semi-buoyant and float downstream. Juvenile development is pelagic for the first few days. Can reach 150 mm in the first year and 430 mm by age five.

Conservation status: Rarer in its natural river environment of the Murray-Darling Basin in recent years, golden perch have benefited greatly from stocking in lakes and impoundments. The greatest threats to the species come from river management and the construction of dams and weirs that hinder the migration of juveniles. Recently listed as part of a threatened fish community in the lower Murray River.

Fishing: Golden perch are a prized inland angling species that is taken in a wide variety of locations and by every angling method allowed. At its best in its natural river environment, golden perch eagerly attack lures and baits presented close to large snags by persistent anglers. In lakes the species grows large and excessively fat, but can still be taken on lures, baits and flies. The most interesting fishing development for the golden perch is polarising lake edges and weedy bays for cruising golden perch.

Eating: Its fine eating qualities, when small, make them an ideal and much sought after recreational fishing species.

PERCH, JUNGLE

Scientific name: *Kuhlia rupestris.* Also known as Rock flagtail.
Similar species: Not likely to be confused with other species.

Description: A large eye and large mouth with a slightly convex head profile. A moderate sized fish that is somewhat laterally flattened.

Jungle perch have a distinctive black blotch on the upper and lower lobes of the tail. Brown to olive on the back, grading to a silvery belly. Many brown to red spots cover the entire body.

Life cycle: Highly active and inquisitive, jungle perch need access to saltwater to complete their breeding cycle. The sperm can only survive in a saline environment. Breeding commonly occurs in early summer when water temperatures rise and there is higher rainfall. Juveniles make long migration runs back to fresh water during January and February when 10–20 mm in length.

Conservation status: Considered extremely rare due to the manipulation of rivers for farming. The jungle perch requires clean water for survival with unrestricted access to estuaries to complete its breeding cycle.

Fishing: Jungle perch can be caught on lures and flies fished in the clear rainforest streams of northern Australia. Often located below a major rapid, jungle perch can be seen in the water because of the distinctive tail blotches. Aggressive and inquisitive, jungle perch will eat or attack almost any offering, but are most fun to target on surface lures and flies.

Eating: Jungle perch should not be taken for the table as they are rare in their natural environment.

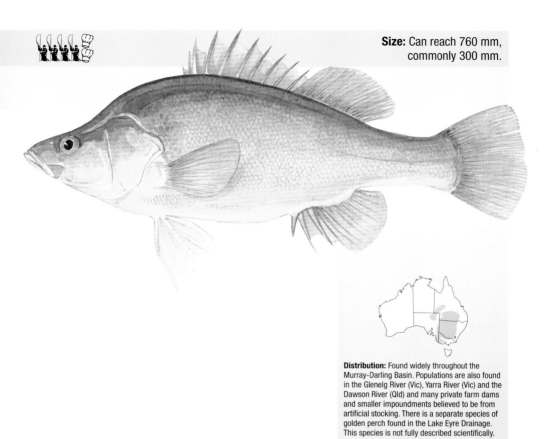

Distribution: Found widely throughout the Murray-Darling Basin. Populations are also found in the Glenelg River (Vic), Yarra River (Vic) and the Dawson River (Qld) and many private farm dams and smaller impoundments believed to be from artificial stocking. There is a separate species of golden perch found in the Lake Eyre Drainage. This species is not fully described scientifically.

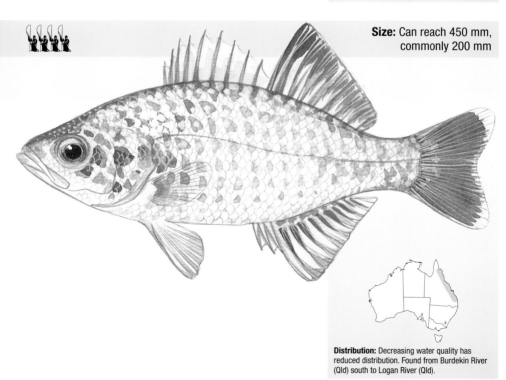

Size: Can reach 450 mm, commonly 200 mm

Distribution: Decreasing water quality has reduced distribution. Found from Burdekin River (Qld) south to Logan River (Qld).

PERCH, MACQUARIE

Scientific name: *Macquaria australasica.* Also known as Mountain perch, Silver eye, Black bream, Macca.
Similar species: Golden perch *Macquaria ambigua.*

Description: A moderate sized fish that is oval and laterally compressed. Head profile is concave with a rounded snout. Eyes are large and prominent, commonly with a very distinct white iris. Jaws are equal length and lips are large without being excessively so. Colour varies with environment, but commonly slate grey or black.

Life cycle: Macquarie perch breed from October through to December when water temperatures rise above 16ºC. Males breed at two years of age and 210 mm, females at three and 300 mm. Spawning occurs in rifles between depths of 50–75 cm with females laying 32,000 eggs per kilogram of body weight.

Conservation status: River regulation and development have restricted and reduced the Macquarie perch's range. The species is fully protected in New South Wales and Victoria has very tight controls on fishing for the species. The species is listed as endangered by the Australian Society for Fish Biology.

Fishing: Macquarie perch are best targeted using worms or shrimp fished on or near the bottom. Timid biters that taste and test a bait before committing, they are a strong fighter once hooked. Often located in schools, it is easy to catch more than the bag limit of fish. Can also be caught on small minnow-style lures and mudeye pattern flies when conditions are suitable.

Eating: Macquarie perch are excellent eating, but its low numbers and strong regulations mean anglers should consider releasing the entire catch.

PERCH, OXLEYAN PYGMY

Scientific name: *Nannoperca oxleyana.*
Similar species: Other pygmy perches.

Description: A moderately compressed body with a small mouth and slight concave head profile. Dorsal fin set well back. Head dominated by large eye.

Light brown to olive on the back with paler sides. A conspicuous black spot near the base of the tail.

Life cycle: Prefers still or slow flowing environments with plenty of cover. Spawns from October to May when temperatures exceed 20ºC. Fish are mature at 4–5 months.

Conservation status: Habitat alteration has geographically restricted the species to limited locations with all populations being relatively small in number. The species is listed as endangered by the Australian Society for Fish Biology. A recovery management plan has been prepared for the species.

Fishing: Due to its low numbers, anglers should not target this species.

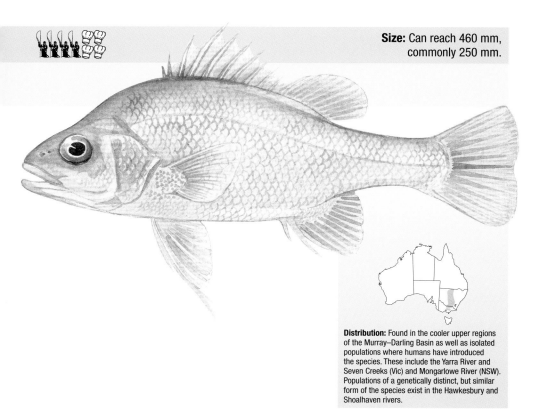

Distribution: Found in the cooler upper regions of the Murray–Darling Basin as well as isolated populations where humans have introduced the species. These include the Yarra River and Seven Creeks (Vic) and Mongarlowe River (NSW). Populations of a genetically distinct, but similar form of the species exist in the Hawkesbury and Shoalhaven rivers.

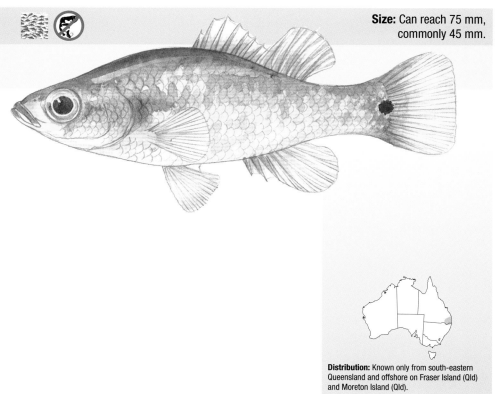

Size: Can reach 75 mm, commonly 45 mm.

Distribution: Known only from south-eastern Queensland and offshore on Fraser Island (Qld) and Moreton Island (Qld).

PERCH, REDFIN

Scientific name: *Perca fluviatilis.* Also known as English perch, Reddie, European perch.
Similar species: Golden perch *Macquaria ambigua,* Silver Perch juveniles *Bidyanus bidyanus.*

Description: A deep bodied fish with a humped back and sail like first dorsal fin that is clearly separated from the second dorsal fin. Large head and mouth and tough, large scales that are firmly implanted in the skin.

Colour varies from an olive green to grey on the back, fading to green or silver on the flanks and silver/white on the belly. Flanks dominated by six or more vertical bands. Juveniles are more slender and may lack the vertical bands.

Life cycle: Prefers slow flowing water with a lot of aquatic vegetation. Spawning occurs in spring over weed and timber with females laying several hundred thousand eggs in a long ribbon. Eggs hatch in 1–3 weeks, depending on temperature.

Males mature at age one, females can take up to four years to mature.

Conservation status: Widely distributed and under no conservation threat.

Fishing: Anglers easily take redfin on jigs, lures, flies and baits. They are an aggressive, schooling fish that are very competitive towards food.

Eating: Excellent as table fair, redfin are considered one of, if not the best food fish in southern freshwater regions.

PERCH, SILVER

Scientific name: *Bidyanus bidyanus.* Also known as Grunter, Murray perch, Black bream, Silver bream, Bidyan.
Similar species: Welch's grunter *Bidyanus welchi,* Barcoo grunter *Scortum barcoo.*

Description: A moderate sized fish with compressed body. Small head and eyes with small beak like mouth in larger specimens. Dorsal fin has hard spines at front and is soft towards the tail. Tail slightly forked. Small scales. Colour varies from almost black in clear water to silvery grey to greenish gold in dirty water and even a creamy white.

Life cycle: Occurs mainly in areas of moderate to high flow. Spawns in spring and summer after migration upstream. Moderately fecund, a female can release up to 300,000 eggs that are semi-buoyant. Males mature at age three and 250 mm, females at age five and 290 mm. Has been recorded at 27 years of age.

Conservation status: Considered rare and listed as vulnerable by the Australian Society for Fish Biology in the natural riverine environment, silver perch are protected and may not be taken. In stocked impoundments, silver perch grow large and can be targeted by anglers.

Fishing: Silver perch are a difficult fish to target when they are at a large size, however smaller fish will attack baits with vigour until hooked. Best baits include worms, shrimps and small wood grubs fished on a running sinker rig or paternoster rig. Can be targeted by anglers using small spinning or diving lures as well as yabby and shrimp imitation flies over shallow, grassy banks in impoundments.

Be aware of the current fishing regulations as silver perch are protected in rivers in many states.

Size: Can reach 600 mm, commonly 300 mm.

Distribution: An introduced exotic species that is widespread in south-eastern Australia on both sides of the Great Dividing Range. Also present in Tasmania and the south-western corner of Western Australia.

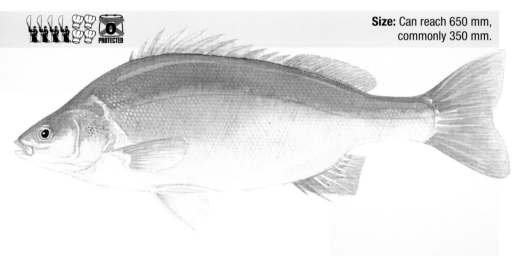

Size: Can reach 650 mm, commonly 350 mm.

Distribution: Natural range includes most waters of the Murray-Darling Basin excluding the high altitude, cold head waters. Has been introduced into many east coast drainages and lakes for recreational fishing.

PERCH, SOUTHERN PYGMY

Scientific name: *Nannoperca australis.* Also known as Pygmy perch.
Similar species: Other pygmy perches.

Description: Moderately compressed body with a small mouth and large eye. Dorsal fin situated well back, tail slightly rounded. Colour is highly variable with geography and water clarity. Base colours vary from pale green to green brown that is darker on the dorsal surface and almost white on the ventral surface. Dark splotches and blotches along the flanks that are highly variable among individuals. Females are never as colourful as males.

Life cycle: Most common in slower flowing waters with abundant cover where the species forms loose schools. Most populations are dominated by 1–2 year olds, but the species can live to five years of age. Both sexes mature at age one with breeding occurring between September and January. Females produce between 100 and 600 eggs with body size being a dictating factor.

Conservation status: The range of the species has been drastically reduced since European settlement, however, where the species occurs, populations are stable.

Fishing: Not recommended as an angling species.

PERCH, SPANGLED

Scientific name: *Leiopotherapon unicolor.* Also known as Jewel perch, Bobby cod.
Similar species: Large-scaled grunter *Leiopotherapon macrolepsis.*

Description: A small to moderate size fish with a large head and moderate size eyes. A rounded snout sits atop a large mouth. Dorsal fin almost separated with spines towards the front and rays towards the rear of the fish. Colour varies with locality but commonly brown to steely blue on the dorsal surface, gold to silver on the flanks and white on the belly. Flanks are marked with brownish red spots.

Life cycle: Completes its entire life cycle in fresh water with spawning occurring during November. A highly fecund species that is one of the few species capable of breeding in still water impoundments. Known to be a schooling species, it has been reported that the species can aestivate (survive in bottom mud) when water holes dry up, although there is no published evidence of this. It is one of the first species to colonise re-flooded lakes and wetlands.

Conservation status: Abundant in many locations.

Fishing: Readily attacks baits meant for other species, but rarely targeted by anglers due to its small average size. Can be taken on small lures and flies.

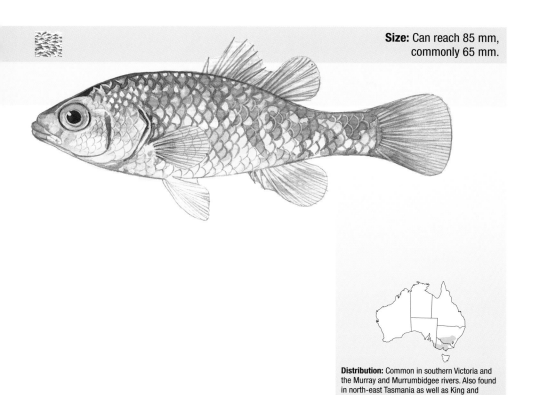

Size: Can reach 85 mm, commonly 65 mm.

Distribution: Common in southern Victoria and the Murray and Murrumbidgee rivers. Also found in north-east Tasmania as well as King and Flinders islands.

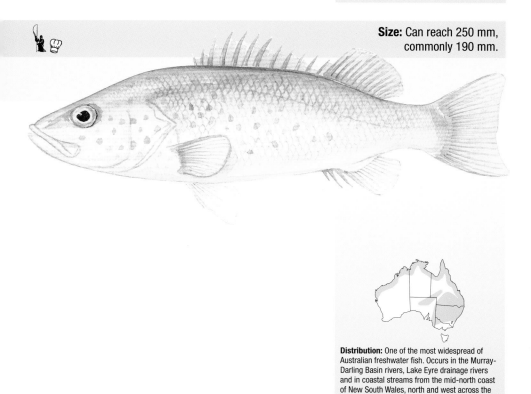

Size: Can reach 250 mm, commonly 190 mm.

Distribution: One of the most widespread of Australian freshwater fish. Occurs in the Murray-Darling Basin rivers, Lake Eyre drainage rivers and in coastal streams from the mid-north coast of New South Wales, north and west across the Top End and in many rivers on the West Coast.

PERCH, YARRA PIGMY

Scientific name: *Nannoperca obscura*.
Similar species: Other pygmy perches.

Description: Moderately compressed body with moderate eye and small mouth. A dusky pale brown colour with a paler belly. Spots along the midline with an indistinct bar across the caudal peduncle. Males often have brighter coloration than females, especially around spawning periods.

Life cycle: Inhabits heavily vegetated streams and often found in small schools. Believed to breed in September and October when males are 35 mm long and females 40 mm in length.

Conservation status: Limited distribution means populations are fragmented and the species is at risk of extinction.

Fishing: Listed under the Victorian Flora and Fauna Guarantee Act 1988 and may not be taken in Victoria.

PERCHLET, ESTUARY

Scientific name: *Ambassis marianus*. Also known as Silver perchlet, Convex perchlet.
Similar species: Olive perchlet *Ambassis agassizii*, juvenile Golden perch *Macquaria ambigua*, juvenile Redfin *Perca fluviatilis*.

Description: A small species with a compressed oval body and a moderately large mouth and very large eye. Dorsal fin divided by a deep notch and tail heavily forked. A semi-transparent species that has dusky scale edges.

Life cycle: Small to large aggregations of the species are common in coastal drainages and the lower portions of the freshwater feeder creeks and streams. Very little else is known of their life history.

Conservation status: Abundant throughout its natural range.

Fishing: Can be collected in dip nets and drag nets in estuaries, but due to its small size is rarely targeted by anglers.

PERCHLET, MACLEAY'S

Scientific name: *Ambassis macleayi*.
Similar species: Olive perchlet *Ambassis agassizii*.

Description: A laterally compressed body with a small head and large eye above amoderate mouth. Dorsal fins separated and tail heavily forked. Dark silver in appearance and scales have dark fringes giving a net like appearance. Commonly, a dark blotch is present at the base of the tail.

Life cycle: Very little is known.

Conservation status: Common along the west coast of the Cape York Peninsula, less common on the east coast.

Fishing: Not targeted by anglers.

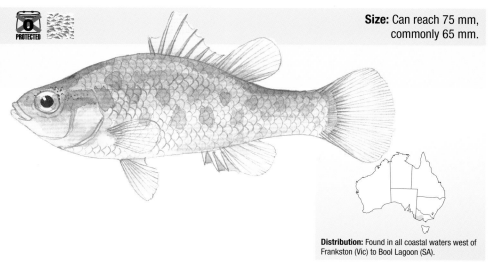

Size: Can reach 75 mm, commonly 65 mm.

Distribution: Found in all coastal waters west of Frankston (Vic) to Bool Lagoon (SA).

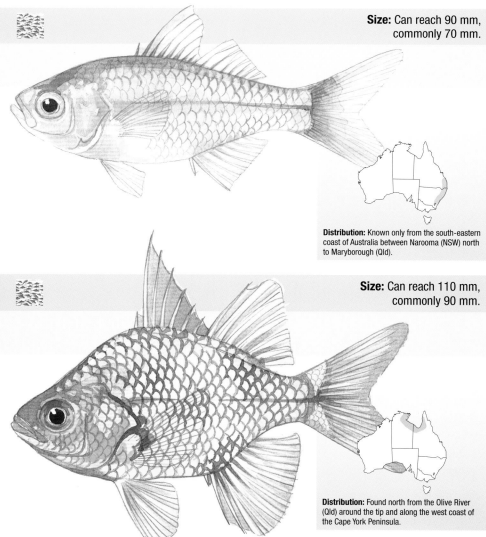

Size: Can reach 90 mm, commonly 70 mm.

Distribution: Known only from the south-eastern coast of Australia between Narooma (NSW) north to Maryborough (Qld).

Size: Can reach 110 mm, commonly 90 mm.

Distribution: Found north from the Olive River (Qld) around the tip and along the west coast of the Cape York Peninsula.

PERCHLET, OLIVE

Scientific name: *Ambassis agassizii*. Also known as Silver spray, Agassiz's glassfish.
Similar species: Estuary perchlet *Ambassis marianus*, juvenile Golden perch *Macquaria ambigua*, juvenile Redfin *Perca fluviatilis*.

Description: An oval, laterally compressed body with moderate sized mouth and a very large eye. Dorsal fin divided by a deep notch and tail slightly forked. Scales fringed by dark pigment giving a net like appearance. Generally semi-transparent with clear fins.

Life cycle: Small to large aggregations are occasionally found where heavy vegetation is present. Spawning occurs in November and December with a 5 cm female being recorded having 2,300 eggs.

Conservation status: Relatively common throughout its natural range.

Fishing: Too small to be of interest to anglers.

PLATY

Scientific name: *Xiphophorus maculatus*.
Similar species: Guppy *Poecilia reticulata*.

Description: A small species with a compressed, deep body. Dorsal fin located high on arched back. Small head with small mouth and moderate eye. Tail slightly rounded and caudal peduncle thick. Males are smaller than females. Colour is plain brownish olive, however irregular blotches and red stripes can appear on the flanks.

Life cycle: An introduced aquarium species that bears live young. Breeds in spring and autumn and may breed more than once a season.

Conservation status: Introduced exotic species.

Fishing: Can be taken in dip nets, but should not be kept alive or transported to any other waterway.

RAINBOWFISH, BLACK BANDED

Scientific name: *Melanotaenia nigrans*.
Similar species: Other Rainbowfish.

Description: A small species that is not as brightly coloured as other rainbowfish. Large eye, small mouth and pointed snout with a slightly forked tail. Long second dorsal and anal fins. Almost semi-transparent, fins are pale yellow and a distinctive black stripe runs along each flank.

Life cycle: Breeding occurs throughout the year with a peak in the warmer months leading up to the wet season. Little else is known.

Conservation status: Abundant throughout its natural range.

Fishing: Too small to be of interest to anglers.

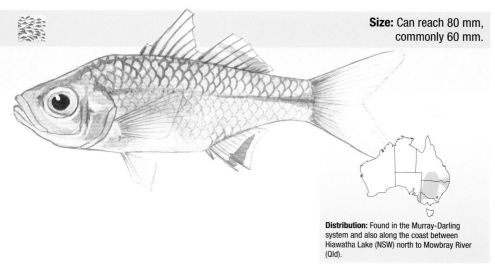

Size: Can reach 80 mm, commonly 60 mm.

Distribution: Found in the Murray-Darling system and also along the coast between Hiawatha Lake (NSW) north to Mowbray River (Qld).

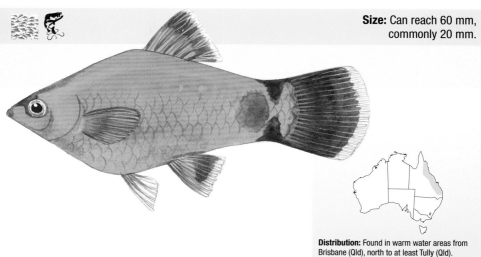

Size: Can reach 60 mm, commonly 20 mm.

Distribution: Found in warm water areas from Brisbane (Qld), north to at least Tully (Qld).

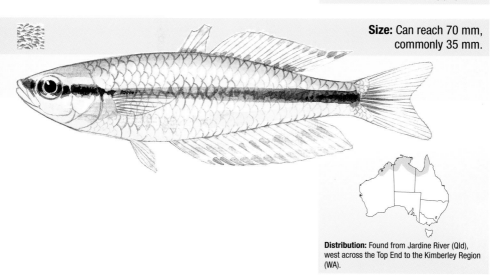

Size: Can reach 70 mm, commonly 35 mm.

Distribution: Found from Jardine River (Qld), west across the Top End to the Kimberley Region (WA).

RAINBOWFISH, CAIRNS

Scientific name: *Cairnsichthys rhombosomoides.*
Similar species: Other Rainbowfish.

Description: An elongate fish with a tapered snout and a large eye. Plainly coloured with a brown back fading to a white or cream on the belly. There is a dark band running down the length of the flanks and the anal fin has a dark margin.

Life cycle: Believed to breed all year with a peak during the wet season. Little else is known.

Conservation status: Common in its natural range, but limited distribution means the species is listed as vulnerable by the Australian Society for Fish Biology.

Fishing: Too small to be of interest to anglers.

RAINBOWFISH, CHECKERED

Scientific name: *Melanotaenia splendida inornata.* Also known as Murray-Darling sunfish, Pink-ear.
Similar species: Other Rainbowfish.

Description: A deep bodied and laterally compressed rainbowfish with a pointed head and a large eye. Tail with a shallow fork. Large anal fin and second dorsal fin. Yellow or orange stripes along the back half of the body and coloured fins give a chequered appearance.

Life cycle: Very little is known.

Conservation status: Common throughout most of its natural range, although increasingly rare in the southern Murray-Darling Basin.

Fishing: Too small to be of interest to anglers.

RAINBOWFISH, CRIMSON SPOTTED

Scientific name: *Melanotaenia fluviatilis.* Also known as Murray River rainbowfish.
Similar species: Other Rainbowfish.

Description: Slender and compressed in the body with a moderate head and large eye. Two dorsal fins separated by a gap and large anal fin, tail slightly forked. Silvery gold in colour with a green iridescence fading to whitish on the belly. Males more brightly coloured than females.

Life cycle: Spawning is seasonal in the lower catchment areas with females laying several eggs a day for the male to fertilise. Cool water temperature appears to limit the distribution and breeding success.

Conservation status: Common throughout its natural range.

Fishing: Too small to be of interest to anglers.

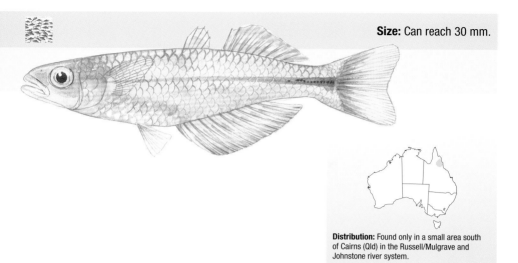

Size: Can reach 30 mm.

Distribution: Found only in a small area south of Cairns (Qld) in the Russell/Mulgrave and Johnstone river system.

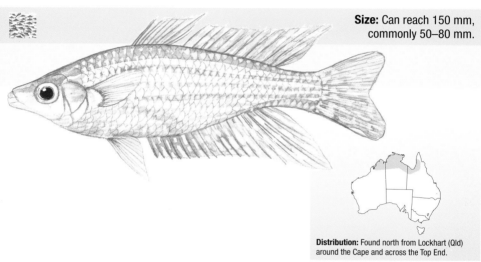

Size: Can reach 150 mm, commonly 50–80 mm.

Distribution: Found north from Lockhart (Qld) around the Cape and across the Top End.

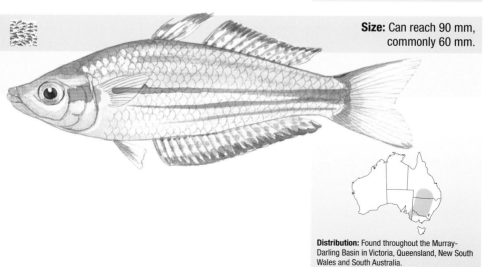

Size: Can reach 90 mm, commonly 60 mm.

Distribution: Found throughout the Murray-Darling Basin in Victoria, Queensland, New South Wales and South Australia.

RAINBOWFISH, DUBOULAY'S

Scientific name: *Melanotaenia duboulayi.* Also known as Common or Spotted sunfish.
Similar species: Other Rainbowfish.

Description: A slender and compressed body with a moderate size head and large eye. Two dorsal fins separated by a gap. In males the first dorsal can reach the second dorsal fin. Tail is slightly forked. Underlying colour is olive brown on the back to silvery green on the flanks. Most scales have a dark fringe and there is narrow reddish stripe between each row of scales.

Life cycle: Inhabits many different environments including lakes, ponds, rivers, creeks and irrigation ditches. Lays small batches of eggs over successive days that are fertilised by the male and hatch after a week.

Conservation status: Common throughout its natural range.

Fishing: Too small to be of interest to anglers.

RAINBOWFISH, McCULLOCH'S

Scientific name: *Melanttaenia maccullochi.*
Similar species: Other Rainbowfish.

Description: An elongate and laterally compressed body with a small head and dominant large eye. Tail slightly forked and dorsal fins separated by a gap. Large anal fin. Base colour is olive brown on the back, fading to white on the ventral surface. Flanks are lined with 6–9 dark stripes.

Life cycle: Breeding believed to occur throughout the year when conditions are suitable, but believed to have a peak during the build up to the wet season.

Conservation status: Common throughout its natural range.

Fishing: Too small to be of interest to anglers.

RAINBOWFISH, SOFTSPINED

Scientific name: *Rhadinocentrus ornatus.* Also known as Ornate rainbowfish, Sunfish, Jewelfish, Neon sunfish.
Similar species: Other Rainbowfish.

Description: A slender and compressed species with a moderate sized head and a large eye. Two dorsal fins are separated by a gap and the tail is slightly forked. Patterns and colours vary according to location but usually translucent, light brown or bluish. Scales have a heavy dark fringe.

Life cycle: Commonly found in swamp country with slow flowing or stagnant water. Lays small batches of eggs over successive days that are fertilised by the male and hatch after a week.

Conservation status: Common throughout its natural range.

Fishing: Too small to be of interest to anglers

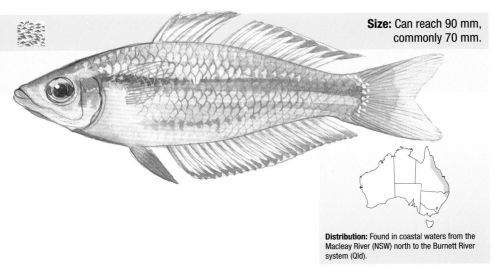

Size: Can reach 90 mm, commonly 70 mm.

Distribution: Found in coastal waters from the Macleay River (NSW) north to the Burnett River system (Qld).

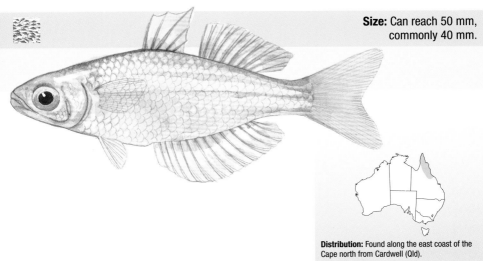

Size: Can reach 50 mm, commonly 40 mm.

Distribution: Found along the east coast of the Cape north from Cardwell (Qld).

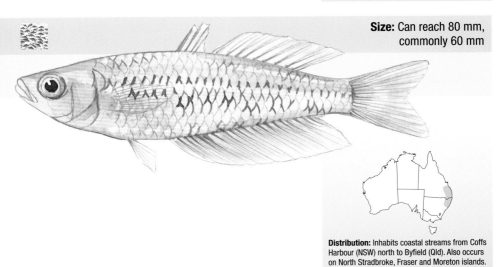

Size: Can reach 80 mm, commonly 60 mm

Distribution: Inhabits coastal streams from Coffs Harbour (NSW) north to Byfield (Qld). Also occurs on North Stradbroke, Fraser and Moreton islands.

RAINBOWFISH, THREADFIN

Scientific name: *Iriatherina werneri.*
Similar species: Other Rainbowfish.

Description: A narrow and shallow body shape with a pointed head and large eye. Males have greatly enlarged dorsal and anal fins and the top and bottom lobes of the tail can also be enlarged. The body is usually silver, but can have light bars.

Life cycle: Believed to breed all year with a peak during the wet season. Little else is known.

Conservation status: Common throughout its natural range.

Fishing: Too small to be of interest to anglers.

ROACH

Scientific name: *Rutilis rutilis.*
Similar species: Carp *Cyprinus carpio.*

Description: Deep bodied, but occasionally slender (as in Lake Eildon population) with a high, arched back and a small head, moderate eye and small mouth. Single dorsal fin and tail forked. Olive green on the dorsal surface fading to silver on the flanks and silvery white on the belly. Dorsal fin and tail usually dark, while the pectoral fins can be orange or orange red. Eyes are distinctly bright red.

Life cycle: A day active fish that spawns among vegetation during lengthening spring days. Larvae take 2–3 weeks to hatch.

Conservation status: An introduced species that is common where it occurs.

Fishing: Can be targeted by using coarse fishing methods. Small baits like maggots and corn can bring excellent results with judicious use of berley. Can also be taken on small flies when the fish are seen rising to hatching midge.

SALMON, ATLANTIC

Scientific name: *Salmo salar.*
Similar species: Particularly Brown trout *Salmo trutta,* but also other trouts and salmons.

Description: Closely resembles brown trout. Body elongate, head moderate and eye small. One dorsal fin plus adipose fin on dorsal surface. Caudal peduncle has a narrow wrist that is smaller than brown trout's and the tail is more deeply forked. Colour varies from black blue to silvery blue with dark x-shaped splotches. In lakes the species can become metallic silver in colour. A clear distinction with brown trout is that Atlantic salmon lack teeth along the midline of the roof of the mouth.

Life cycle: There is no known natural breeding population in Australia. All known populations are the result of artificial stocking or escaped individuals from fish farms.

Conservation status: Numbers are dependent on stocking rates and environmental factors.

Fishing: Atlantic salmon are favoured for their great fighting abilities and are targeted by anglers using all legal fishing methods. The most challenging way to target this species is with fly fishing gear in the estuaries of southern Tasmania. Small minnow pattern flies work best early morning and into the evening. Trolling lures in lakes, or casting small minnow lures where the species is present can also be rewarding.

Eating: The Atlantic salmon makes excellent table fare and is well suited to all cooking methods.

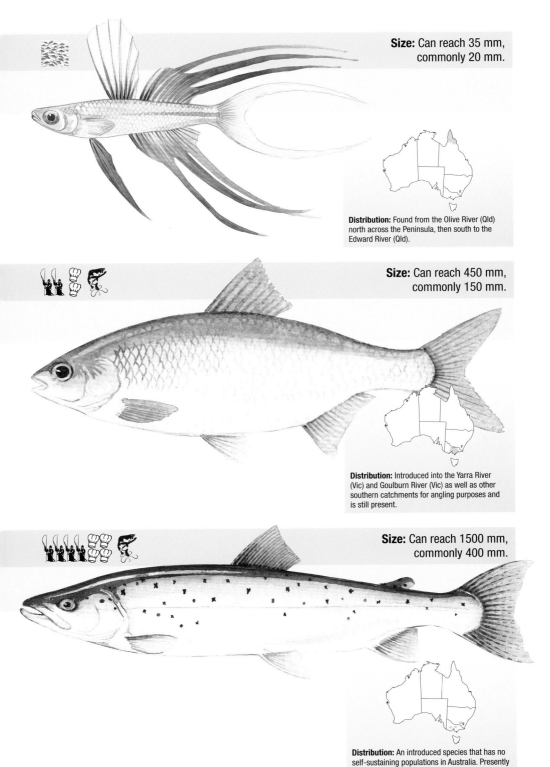

Size: Can reach 35 mm, commonly 20 mm.

Distribution: Found from the Olive River (Qld) north across the Peninsula, then south to the Edward River (Qld).

Size: Can reach 450 mm, commonly 150 mm.

Distribution: Introduced into the Yarra River (Vic) and Goulburn River (Vic) as well as other southern catchments for angling purposes and is still present.

Size: Can reach 1500 mm, commonly 400 mm.

Distribution: An introduced species that has no self-sustaining populations in Australia. Presently stocks are liberated into lakes Jindabyne (NSW), Bullen Merri (Vic) and in some waters in Tasmania where it is heavily farmed. Escapees from hatcheries are often caught from the Goulburn River (Vic).

SALMON, CHINOOK

Scientific name: *Oncorhynchus tshawytscha.* Also known as Quinnat salmon, King salmon.
Similar species: All other trout and salmon species.

Description: Generally trout like but with a more pointed snout and a slightly larger mouth. Colour is predominantly silvery with a dark green or black back and occasionally small black spots along the top of the flanks. Inside the mouth can be coloured dark grey or black around teeth in the lower jaw.

Life cycle: No natural breeding population exists in Australia and populations are maintained by stocking.

Conservation status: Numbers are dependent on stocking rates and environmental factors.

Fishing: Chinook salmon are considered great fighters and are targeted by anglers using all legal fishing methods. The most challenging way to target this species is with fly fishing gear in the stocked lakes using small minnow pattern flies. Trolling lures in the same lakes, or casting small minnow lures from the bank or boats can also be rewarding. The most effective method is to berley (where legal) with minced pilchard, then fish pilchard fillets or small whitebait under floats or close to the bottom in the berley trail.

Eating: The Chinook salmon makes excellent table fare and is well suited to all cooking methods.

SARATOGA, GULF

Scientific name: *Scleropages jardinii.* Also known as Northern saratoga.
Similar species: Southern saratoga *Scleropages leichardti.*

Description: A rather long and slender species that has large pectoral fins and large scales. The mouth is upturned, oblique and very bony with two barbels on the chin, while the eye is of moderate size. Body colour is generally silver, but each scale is adorned with an orange-pink shape that can appear as spots.

Life cycle: Studies suggest females mature at age five and at approximately 430 mm in length. Breeding takes place in October and November when water temperatures exceed 23°C. The females are buccal incubators, holding the eggs in their mouths until they hatch. The young use the mother's mouth as a safe refuge when danger approaches.

Conservation status: Common throughout its natural range although anecdotal reports suggest numbers are dropping.

Fishing: The gulf saratoga is a surface to mid-water feeder that can be targeted by anglers fishing baits, lures and flies near or on the surface. The most exciting way to target the species is with surface lures or flies fished slowly amongst heavy cover such as lily pads. Slow, jerky retrieves often bring about spectacular surface strikes. The species can be targeted by fishing small baits such as cherabin or small mullet under floats in the vicinity of structure.

An excellent fighting fish, the gulf saratoga is eagerly sought by many sport fishers.

Eating: Unlike their respected fighting prowess, the saratoga has a reputation of being a poor eating fish and most fish are released without delay.

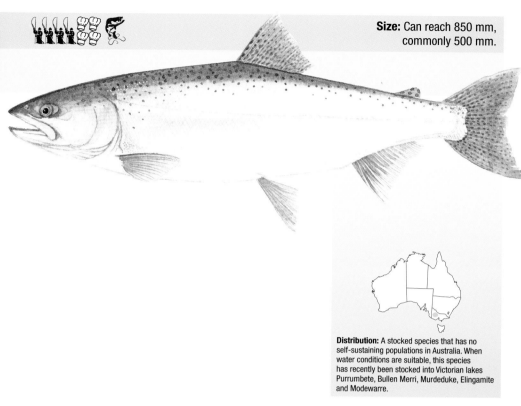

Size: Can reach 850 mm, commonly 500 mm.

Distribution: A stocked species that has no self-sustaining populations in Australia. When water conditions are suitable, this species has recently been stocked into Victorian lakes Purrumbete, Bullen Merri, Murdeduke, Elingamite and Modewarre.

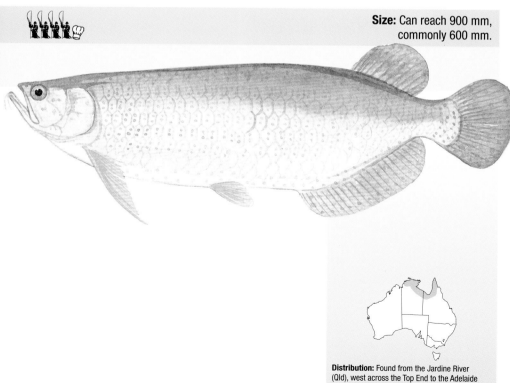

Size: Can reach 900 mm, commonly 600 mm.

Distribution: Found from the Jardine River (Qld), west across the Top End to the Adelaide River (NT).

SARATOGA, SOUTHERN

Scientific name: *Scleropages leichardti.* Also known as Spotted barramundi, Leichardt saratoga, Dawson River salmon.
Similar species: Gulf saratoga *Scleropagus jardinii.*

Description: A rather long and slender species that has large pectoral fins and large scales. The mouth is upturned, oblique and very bony with two barbels on the chin, while the eye is of moderate size. Body colour is generally silver, but each scale is adorned with an orange-pink shape that can appear as spots.

Life cycle: Breeding is believed to start at age five when fish reach approximately 360 mm in length. Spawning takes place in September and October when water temperatures are between 20° and 23°C. Saratoga are buccal incubators, which means the female incubates the eggs in her mouth until they hatch. For up to three days after the fry hatch they flee to the mother's mouth for safety when threatened.

Conservation status: In their natural range numbers are low, but artificial breeding of the species and stocking in other waterways has seen individual numbers of fish increase. Listed by the Australian Society of Fish Biology as lower-risk, near threatened.

Fishing: The southern saratoga is a surface to mid-water feeder that is targeted by anglers fishing baits, lures and flies near or on the surface. The most exciting way to target the species is with surface lures or flies fished slowly amongst heavy cover such as lily pads in stocked impoundments. Slow, jerky retrieves are rewarded with spectacular surface strikes and hard fighting.

An excellent fighting fish, the southern saratoga is eagerly sought by many sport fishers in waters where it has been stocked.

Eating: This species has a reputation of being a poor eating fish and most, if not all, fish are released without delay.

SAWFISH, FRESHWATER

Scientific name: *Pristis zijsron.* Also known as Green sawfish.
Similar species: Other Marine sawfish.

Description: A large species that is immediately recognisable due to the large saw-like nose on the front of the head. Teeth adorn this elongated and flattened snout and are believed to be used for hunting and in the mating ritual. A member of the shark and ray family, the sawfish has a skeleton of cartilage and its body is flattened and similar in shape to many bottom dwelling sharks. Colour generally varies from light sandy brown to a darker brown with a white ventral surface.

Life cycle: Sawfish are believed to breed in fresh water and young are born live with a gelatinous covering over the already formed saw. Little else is known.

Conservation status: Found in deeper and larger systems with mud or sand bottoms, but is listed as endangered by the Australian Society of Fish Biology.

Fishing: Not often taken by recreational anglers, however the species has been recorded as being caught on live baits intended for other species.

Eating: The flesh is reported to be excellent eating, but few encounters and their extraordinary appearance normally sees most caught fish released.

Size: Can reach 900 mm, commonly 600 mm.

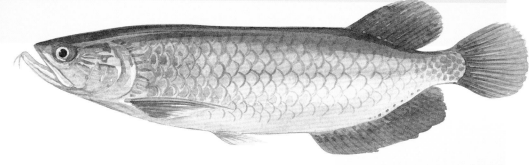

Distribution: Found naturally in the Fitzroy/Dawson River system, but has been introduced into many southern and central Queensland lakes and impoundments.

Size: Can reach 7,000 mm, commonly 5,000 mm.

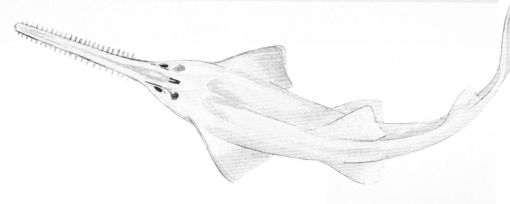

Distribution: Found from Broome (WA), east across the Top End, then south to the Clarence River (NSW).

SHARK, RIVER WHALER

Scientific name: *Carcharhinus leucas*. Also known as Bull shark, River shark, Estuary whaler, Swan River whaler.
Similar species: Other whaler sharks.

Description: These sharks are distinctive because they have short, rounded snouts and very thickset and heavy bodies. Colour varies from almost black to a lighter grey, but general colour is mid-grey.

Life cycle: Very little is known, but young are born free-swimming.

Conservation status: Common throughout their natural range.

Fishing: Can be taken on large baits fished on heavy tackle with the aid of a wire trace and occasionally on lures in clear water.

Eating: The flesh is not considered good eating and the species is rarely targeted.

SILVER BIDDY

Scientific name: *Gerres filamentosus*.
Similar species: None.

Description: Silver biddy are a small silver fish with a long filament extending from the tip of the dorsal fin and a tail that is deeply forked. The species has a small protrusible mouth and a large eye, and they produce copious amounts of slime when captured.

Life cycle: Mainly estuarine but also found in clear streams and flowing water. Very little is known of their breeding.

Conservation status: Common throughout its natural range.

Fishing: Can be taken in cast nets and used for bait to attract larger species such as barramundi. A small fish that does not transport or handle well.

Size: Can reach 3,000 mm, commonly 2,500 mm.

Distribution: Found globally, but in Australia throughout the entire Top End down the east coast to at least the Richmond River (NSW) and down the west coast to at least the Swan River (WA).

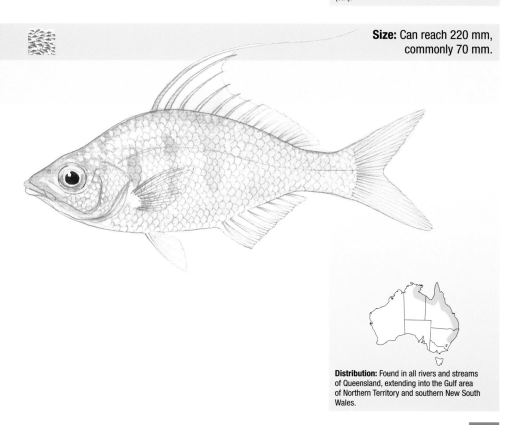

Size: Can reach 220 mm, commonly 70 mm.

Distribution: Found in all rivers and streams of Queensland, extending into the Gulf area of Northern Territory and southern New South Wales.

SMELT, AUSTRALIAN

Scientific name: *Retropinna semoni.*
Similar species: Tasmanian smelt *Retropinna tasmanica.*

Description: A small, slender species with a large eye and a slightly rounded mouth, Australian smelt have a small dorsal fin set well back and a slightly forked tail. At sexual maturity males develop noticeably larger fins. Colour varies from olive on the back to bright silver on the flanks and a silvery-white belly. Fins are generally transparent.

Life cycle: Found in still and slow flowing regions in great abundance. Can spend part of its life at sea, but land-locked populations do not require saltwater. Sexual maturity is reached at age one and life expectancy is only three years. Spawning occurs in water temperatures above 15ºC, with a 55 mm long female producing up to 1,000 eggs.

Conservation status: Abundant throughout its natural range.

Fishing: Not often encountered by anglers and has little value as bait as the fish handles poorly.

SMELT, TASMANIAN

Scientific name: *Retropinna tasmanica.*
Similar species: Australian smelt *Retropinna semoni.*

Description: The Tasmanian smelt is a small compressed fish with a large eye and a pointed snout. The dorsal fin is set well back and the tail is slightly forked. Males develop larger fins at maturity. Colour is bright silver on the flanks with the back darker, tending to be olive on the dorsal surface and the ventral surface is silvery white.

Life cycle: Studied little, but believed to enter rivers along with Tasmanian whitebait as part of the whitebait run. Believed to spawn in the lower reaches of rivers.

Conservation status: Little studied and little known, but believed to be reasonably common.

Fishing: A small and fragile species that does not take handling well. Can be caught when netting whitebait.

SOLE, FRESHWATER

Scientific name: *Brachirus selheimi.*
Similar species: Other estuarine and saltwater sole.

Description: A flattened species with both eyes on one side of the head and appears almost round in shape when viewed from above. Fins extend along almost the entire body length and the colour varies from mottled brown on the top surface to milky white on the bottom surface.

Life cycle: Very little is known, however the eggs are large and sink to the bottom in aquaria.

Conservation status: Believed to be common throughout its natural range.

Fishing: Too small to be of interest to anglers, but occasionally taken on small worm baits meant for other species.

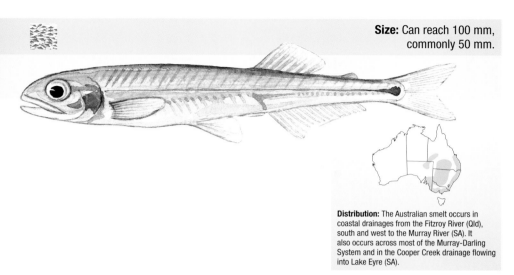

Size: Can reach 100 mm, commonly 50 mm.

Distribution: The Australian smelt occurs in coastal drainages from the Fitzroy River (Qld), south and west to the Murray River (SA). It also occurs across most of the Murray-Darling System and in the Cooper Creek drainage flowing into Lake Eyre (SA).

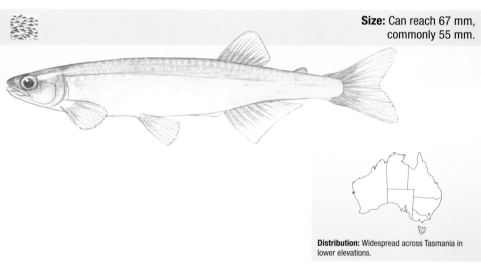

Size: Can reach 67 mm, commonly 55 mm.

Distribution: Widespread across Tasmania in lower elevations.

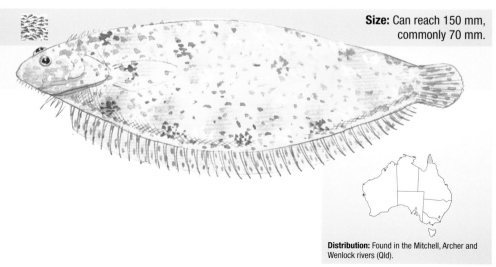

Size: Can reach 150 mm, commonly 70 mm.

Distribution: Found in the Mitchell, Archer and Wenlock rivers (Qld).

SWORDTAIL

Scientific name: *Xiphophorus helleri.*
Similar species: Females may be confused with the Guppy *Poecillia reticulata.*

Description: Deep bodied and laterally compressed with dorsal fin high on arching back. Mouth upturned and protrusible. Moderate eye. Male tail fin elongated at the base to form the distinctive sword-like appearance. Highly variable in colour depending on time spent in the wild. Recent aquarium releases are highly coloured with bright orange fins and alternating silver and orange lines along the flanks. Can revert to dull olive brown with time in wild environments.

Life cycle: Not much studied in Australia, but prefers slow flowing habitats with sparse vegetation. Interestingly females can change sex to males if the need arises in a population.

Conservation status: An exotic introduced species that should not be returned if captured.

Fishing: Too small to be of interest to anglers.

TANDAN, HYRTL'S

Scientific name: *Neosilurus hyrtlii.* Also known as Mottled tandan, White tandan, Glencoe tandan, Silver moonfish.
Similar species: Central Australian catfish *Neosilurus argenteus*, Freshwater catfish *Tandanus tandanus.*

Description: An elongate species with a tapering tail and a small, flattened head. A downturned mouth with four pairs of long, slender barbels. A rounded tail and long anal fin. Body colour varies from dark brown to a pale yellow brown depending on habitat. Fins generally yellowish in colour. In aquaria the yellow coloration is often lost.

Life cycle: Little is known, but spawning behaviour appears to be stimulated by flooding with eggs deposited in fast flowing gravely areas. Inhabits a wide variety of habitats from artesian bores and stagnant pools to streams.

Conservation status: Common throughout its natural range.

Fishing: Not often encountered by anglers, but can be taken on worm and yabby baits occasionally by anglers.

Eating: Larger specimens are considered reasonable eating.

TANDAN, RENDAHL'S

Scientific name: *Porochilus rendahli.*
Similar species: Other eel-tailed catfish.

Description: This small species has a small and pointed head. The mouth is moderate and the eye is relatively large. The tail is rounded and the anal fin is large. Four pairs of barbels adorn the mouth. Colour varies from mottled brown to an all over light tan in murky water.

Life cycle: Very little is known of this small species.

Conservation status: Distribution is patchy and individual numbers are not high.

Fishing: This species is too small to be of interest to anglers.

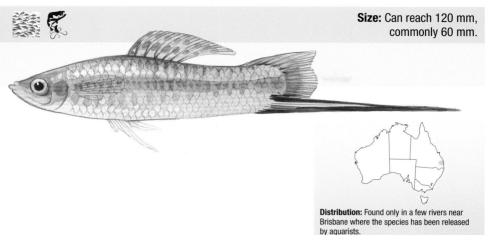

Size: Can reach 120 mm, commonly 60 mm.

Distribution: Found only in a few rivers near Brisbane where the species has been released by aquarists.

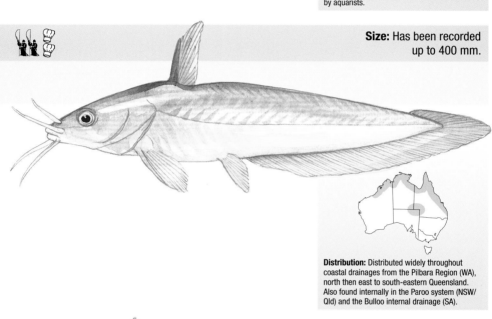

Size: Has been recorded up to 400 mm.

Distribution: Distributed widely throughout coastal drainages from the Pilbara Region (WA), north then east to south-eastern Queensland. Also found internally in the Paroo system (NSW/Qld) and the Bulloo internal drainage (SA).

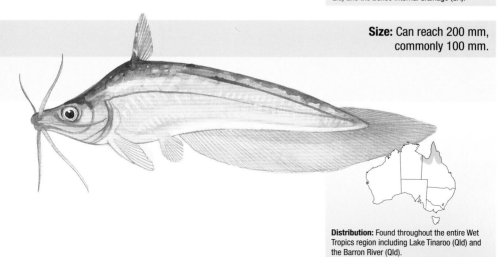

Size: Can reach 200 mm, commonly 100 mm.

Distribution: Found throughout the entire Wet Tropics region including Lake Tinaroo (Qld) and the Barron River (Qld).

TENCH

Scientific name: *Tinca tinca*. Also known as Doctor fish.
Similar species: Carp *Cyprinus carpio*.

Description: A moderately thickset fish with a blunt snout. Small eyes and moderate mouth with a barbel on each corner. Single dorsal fin located on the back. Tail only slightly forked. Colour is commonly olive brown with fins slightly darker. Eyes are a distinctive orange colour.

Life cycle: Inhabits sluggish waters where there is plenty of aquatic weed cover. Spawns most commonly in spring when temperatures reach 15°C or more. Has the ability to spawn more than once in a season.

Conservation status: An introduced species that should not be returned to the water if caught.

Fishing: Coarse fishing methods produce the best results and tench can be attracted to baits by the use of berley. Small hooks with soft baits such as worms or maggots give the best results when fished underneath floats or on the bottom.

Eating: The flesh is said to be firm, white and good to eat.

TROUT, BROOK

Scientific name: *Salvelinus fontinalis*. Also known as Brookie, Brook char, Char.
Similar species: Brown trout *Salmo trutta*, Tiger trout.

Description: A slender and elongated species that closely resemble brown trout. Eye large and mouth lined with teeth. Body has a base olive colour that is darker on the dorsal surface and lighter on the ventral surface. Flanks decorated with spectacular light coloured markings, red spots and orange blotches. Fins can have white fringes near spawning periods.

Life cycle: Breeding is very similar to that of the brown trout where cool, clear water and gravel beds are needed. The species has a tendency to move far upstream into small tributaries and has the ability to mature at very small sizes. Populations in Australia, apart from the New England population and some Tasmanian populations, are maintained by stocking.

Conservation status: An exotic introduced species that is maintained mainly by artificial breeding and stocking.

Fishing: The brook trout can be taken on lures, flies and natural baits such as worms, grasshoppers and crickets. The most difficult and rewarding method to take brook trout is on lure and fly. Any brook trout caught on either of these two methods is considered a great reward for many anglers.

Eating: The brook trout makes excellent table fare having bright orange flesh that suits many different cooking methods.

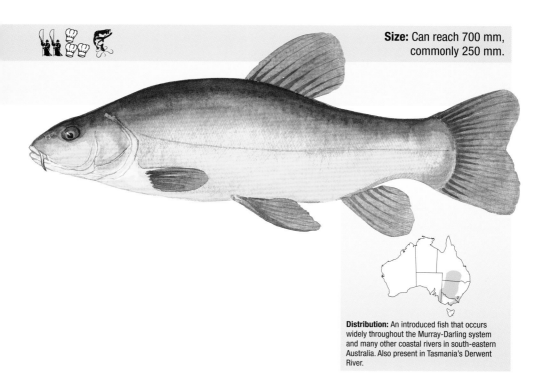

Distribution: An introduced fish that occurs widely throughout the Murray-Darling system and many other coastal rivers in south-eastern Australia. Also present in Tasmania's Derwent River.

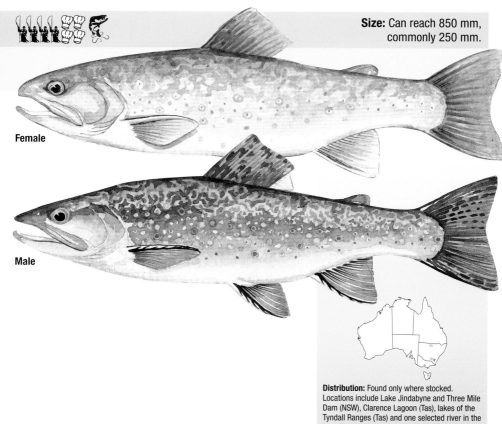

Female

Male

Distribution: Found only where stocked. Locations include Lake Jindabyne and Three Mile Dam (NSW), Clarence Lagoon (Tas), lakes of the Tyndall Ranges (Tas) and one selected river in the New England Region of New South Wales.

TROUT, BROWN

Scientific name: *Salmo trutta.*
Similar species: Brook trout *Salvelinus fontinalis,* Tiger trout.

Description: Brown trout have a large head and mouth, and the eyes are of moderate size. Dorsal fin is located high on the back with a distinctive adipose fin towards the large tail. During spawning males develop a pronounced hooked lower jaw with a distinct upturned tip (kype) that slots neatly into a groove on the top jaw. Colour highly variable and closely related to environment, age and diet. Lake and sea-run fish can appear silver with few spots, while river fish can appear golden brown with many darker spots and occasional red spots with a white halo. In all brown trout the tail is bare of spots and the dorsal fin has many.

Life cycle: Found most commonly in cool water areas. Fish migrate upstream to spawn from April to August, often after a rise in water level associated with heavy rains. Spawning only occurs when the right depth and water velocity occurs over the right gravel substrate. Spawning fish form pairs and the female digs a redd (small depression) with her tail. She then deposits the eggs in the redd and the male moves over the top to fertilise them. The eggs develop over 6–20 weeks, depending on water temperature, and the young alevins spend up to two weeks in the gravel absorbing their yolk sac.

Conservation status: Widespread and abundant throughout its range.

Fishing: Brown trout are one of the most important recreational fishing species in Australia. They are highly regarded because of their growth potential, wariness and occasional difficulty in getting them to strike. They are targeted with bait, lures and flies wherever they occur.

The best times to target brown trout are around dawn and dusk. Large brown trout are well known as nocturnal feeders and these fringe periods of light and dark are most productive for the largest fish.

In rivers, anglers use all methods of fishing successfully. Drifting lightly weighted or unweighted baits is deadly, as is spinning with small minnow lures and bladed spinners in the faster runs and pools. But it is the dry fly fisher that stands to reap the greatest reward by patiently stalking a fish and casting a dry fly or nymph to a sighted fish. This is truly a hunter's game.

In lakes, anglers take brown trout by trolling and casting lures or fly casting along the shores and windlanes. Minnow and crayfish patterns work very well for fly anglers, but midging fish and fish chasing grasshoppers in the shallow lake margins can really get the heart pumping. Bait anglers also find rewards by setting baits such as worms and grubs in shallow water during the evening and into the night.

Eating: The brown trout makes excellent eating with the flesh suitable for all cooking and curing methods.

Lake

River

Distribution: Widely distributed across the south-eastern portion of Australia and Tasmania. Populations also exist in South Australia and the south-western corner of Western Australia.

TROUT, RAINBOW

Scientific name: *Oncorhynchus mykiss*. Also known as Steelhead.
Similar species: Other trout, especially Brown trout juveniles.

Description: A thick-bodied species with a large head and mouth and eyes of moderate size, rainbow trout have a dorsal fin located high on the back and a distinctive adipose fin towards the large tail. During spawning males develop a pronounced hooked lower jaw with a distinct upturned tip (kype) that slots neatly into a groove on the top jaw. The colour is highly variable and closely related to environment, age and diet. Lake and sea-run fish can appear silver with few spots, while river fish can exhibit pink iridescence along the gill covers and flanks. A distinction is that rainbow trout always have spots on their tails and the dorsal fin has many.

Life cycle: Found most commonly in cool water and high altitude areas. Fish migrate upstream to spawn from June to October, often after a rise in water level associated with heavy rains. Spawning only occurs when the right depth and water velocity occurs over the right gravel substrate. Spawning fish form pairs and the female digs a redd (small depression) with her tail. She then deposits the eggs in the redd and the male moves over the top to fertilise them. The eggs develop over 6–20 weeks, depending on water temperature, and the young alevins spend up to two weeks in the gravel absorbing their yolk sac.

Conservation status: Widespread and abundant throughout its range.

Fishing: Rainbow trout are a very important recreational fishing species in Australia. They are highly regarded because of their fighting potential and large size in lakes. They are targeted with bait, lures and flies wherever they occur.

Rainbow trout can be targeted throughout the day and night, but dawn and dusk produce the best results.

In rivers, anglers use all methods of fishing successfully. Drifting lightly weighted or unweighted baits is deadly, as is spinning with small minnow lures and bladed spinners in the faster runs. Fly anglers can also take rainbow trout on nymphs fished through the runs and dry flies fished in faster water.

In lakes, anglers take rainbow trout by trolling and casting lures or fly casting along the shores and windlanes. Minnow and crayfish patterns work very well for fly anglers, but midging rainbow trout generate great challenges. Bait anglers also find rewards by setting baits such as worms and grubs in shallow water during the evening and into thenight.

Eating: The rainbow trout makes excellent eating with the flesh suitable for all cooking and curing methods.

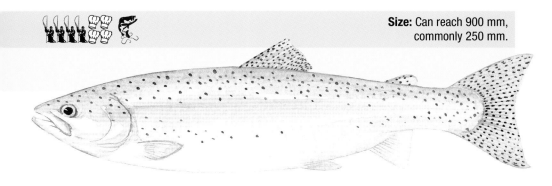

Distribution: Widely distributed across the south-eastern portion of Australia and Tasmania. Populations also exist in South Australia and the south-western corner of Western Australia.

TROUT, TIGER

Scientific name: Not scientifically recognised, as the species is a genetic cross between brook trout and brown trout.
Similar species: Brown trout *Salmo trutta*, Brook trout *Salvelinus fontinalis*.

Description: Tiger trout are a thick-bodied species with a large head and mouth and eyes of moderate size. The dorsal fin is located high on the back with a distinctive adipose fin found towards the large tail. The coloration is distinct with stripes, blotches and patches of yellow, red and undertone of green covering the flanks. Ventral surface lightens, appearing as creamy-white.

Life cycle: Found most commonly in cool water and high altitude areas where stocked. Tiger trout are a sterile species that does not breed.

Conservation status: Density dependent on stocking rates.

Fishing: Tiger trout are a rare, but much sought after recreational fishing species. They are highly regarded because of their rarity and uniqueness. They are targeted with bait, lures and flies wherever they occur.

Tiger trout can be targeted throughout the day and night, but dawn and dusk produce the best results. Anglers use all methods of fishing successfully. Drifting lightly weighted or unweighted baits is deadly, as is spinning with small minnow lures and bladed spinners in the faster runs. Fly anglers can also take tiger trout on nymphs fished through the runs and dry flies fished in faster water. In lakes, anglers take tiger trout trolling and casting lures or fly casting along the shores and near structure. Minnow and crayfish patterns work very well for fly anglers. Bait anglers also find rewards by setting baits such as worms and grubs in shallow water during the evening and into the night.

Eating: Tiger trout make excellent eating with the flesh suitable for all cooking and curing methods.

TUPONG

Scientific name: *Pseudophritis urvilli*. Also known as Congolli, Freshwater flathead, Sand trout.
Similar species: None.

Description: A small to medium fish with an almost cylindrical body, the tupong has a conical head that is slightly flattened on top. The moderate eyes are set high on the head and the mouth is large. Two dorsal fins are clearly separated, with the second being obviously larger. The anal fin is larger than the second dorsal fin and the tail only slightly forked, if at all. Colour is variable and alters with substrate, but the fish is generally a red brown or green brown on the back with irregular markings on the sides and the underside is yellow or white.

Life cycle: Prefers the beds of slow flowing rivers where leaf litter and debris have accumulated. Limited knowledge of spawning patterns, but it is believed that adults migrate to the saltwater for breeding.

Conservation status: Common throughout its natural range.

Fishing: Usually too small to be taken by anglers, however it is taken on soft baits such as worms and small shrimp fished on the bottom.

Eating: The flesh is said to be excellent eating, but the average small size means most individuals caught are released unharmed.

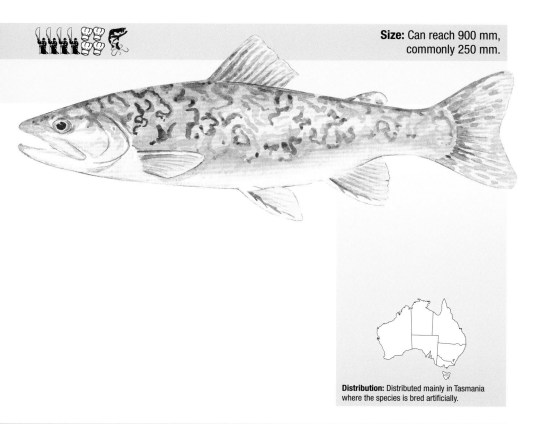

Size: Can reach 900 mm, commonly 250 mm.

Distribution: Distributed mainly in Tasmania where the species is bred artificially.

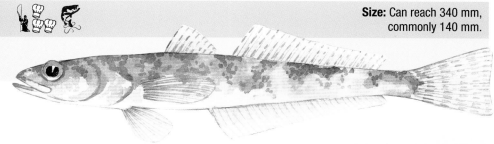

Size: Can reach 340 mm, commonly 140 mm.

Distribution: Found in coastal draining rivers from Bega (NSW) south and then west across the Victorian and South Australian coast, including Tasmania.

WEATHERLOACH, ORIENTAL

Scientific name: *Misgurnus anguillicaudatus.* Also known as Japanese weatherloach, Weatherfish, Mud loach.
Similar species: None.

Description: The Oriental weatherloach has a body that is elongated, cylindrical and sturdy. A single dorsal fin sits mid-way down the body and the tail is rounded. Males are distinguished from females by a larger second ray on the pectoral fin. Colour is generally mottled brown and grey with numerous black spots on the back and sides.

Life cycle: Tolerates a variety of habitats and water conditions with the ability to aestivate over prolonged dry periods. Sexually mature at 100 mm in length, the weatherloach is a multiple spawner that lay between 4,000 and 8,000 eggs per spawning event.

Conservation status: An introduced exotic species that should not be returned to the water.

Fishing: Rarely encountered by anglers but occasionally caught in scoop nets by bait gatherers chasing shrimp and minnow.

YABBY

Scientific name: *Cherax destructor.* Also known as Freshwater crayfish and Craybob.
Similar species: Other decapod crustaceans.

Description: A medium sized freshwater crayfish that is easily distinguished by the large carapace that is fused to all thoracic segments. The tail is segmented and distinct from the thorax. Ten legs or arms are present and are located below the thorax. Colour varies from black, blue grey to light brown or tan and is the result of environment and diet.

Life cycle: Yabbies, like all crustaceans, moult with growth. Water temperature and the availability of food determine the rate of growth and moulting. Yabbies breed when water temperatures rise in spring. A rise in the vicinity of 2°C is all that is required in some populations. The eggs stay attached to the female under the tail and the young are hatched, fully self-sufficient from here.

The yabby can undergo periods of dormancy when water bodies dry, burrowing down into the muds and creating a moist capsule until the next rains moisten the soil enough for the yabby to burrow out.

Conservation status: Common and abundant throughout its natural range

Fishing: Yabbies are most often taken using hoop nets baited with fish off-cuts. These nets are placed near weed beds, deep holes or clay banks and checked every fifteen minutes or so. The species is found profusely in farm dams and here they can be taken using a piece of meat tied to string. The yabby grasps the meat and the angler slowly pulls the yabby to the shallows and runs a landing net underneath it.

Eating: The yabby is one of the finest eating crustaceans available.

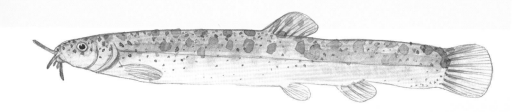

Distribution: Introduced into the Yarra River (Vic) in 1985, the species has spread to colonise the entire system. Also found in the Murray River (NSW/SA), Murrumbidgee River (NSW), Ginninderra Creek (ACT), Lake Eucumbene (NSW) and small suburban waterways around Brisbane (Qld).

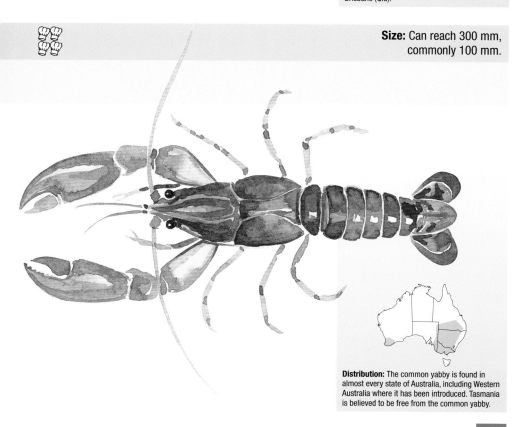

Distribution: The common yabby is found in almost every state of Australia, including Western Australia where it has been introduced. Tasmania is believed to be free from the common yabby.

GLOSSARY

Aestivate: Ability to utilise a period of dormancy to surive warm, dry periods.

Ammocoete: Juvenile stage of lamprey.

Amphidromous: Describes fish that migrate between the sea and fresh water at a regular life-history stage but not directly to spawn.

Anadromous: Describes fish that migrate from the sea anto fresh watex, as adults, to spawn

Billabong: An isolated river pool or backwater.

Carnivore: feeding on other animals.

Catadromous: Describes fish that migrate from fresh water as adults to spawn at sea

Demersal: Living on the bottom.

Detritus: Organic material derived from decomposing animals or plants.

Diadromous: Describes fishes that migrate between fresh and saltwater at a regular life- history phase, in either direction, but not necessarily to spawn.

Diurnal: Active during the day.

Dorsal: The upper surface, back

Endemic: Native and restricted to a given area.

Fecundity: The fertility of a fish, commonly referring to the number of eggs produced by the female.

Gregarious: Tending to live in groups rather than solitary.

Hermaphrodites: Having qualities of both sexes.

Herbivore: Feeds on plants.

Indigenous: Native, although not necessarily restricted, to an area.

Kype: The strongly upturned tip of the mouth in male trouts and salmons.

Larva: The youngest life-history stage.

Lateral: Referring to the sides.

Laterally compressed: Flattened from side to side.

Noxious: Injurious or harmful.

Omnivore: A fish that eats a wide variety of plants and animals.

Operculum: A large bony plate that coves the gills.

Ovoviviparous: Producing young by means of eggs hatched in the body.

Pectoral fins: Paired fins that are lateral, just behind or below the gill openings.

Piscavore: Feeds on fish.

Protrusible: A condition of the jaws where the jaws project forward as a tube when the mouth is open.

Sexual Dimorphism: Different distinguishing features between the females and males in the species.

Ventral: The lower surface, belly.

REFERENCES

Cadwallader P. L. and Backhouse G.N. (1983) *A guide to the Freshwater Fish of Australia*. Victorian Government Printing Office, Melbourne, Australia.

Eussen D. (1997) *Freshwater Fishing Issue 44. Species Guide. Saratoga*. Australian Fishing Network, South Croydon, Australia.

Herbert B. and Peeters J. (1995) *Freshwater Fishes of Far North Queensland*. Publishing Services Department of Primary Industries, Brisbane, Australia.

Lake S. J. (1971) *Freshwater Fishes and Rivers of Austrialia*. Thomas Nelson (Australia) Ltd., Melbourne, Australia.

McDowell R. (Editor) (1996) *Freshwater Fishes of South-Eastern Australia*. Reed Books, Chatswood, Australia.

Merrick J. R. and Scmida G. E. (1984) *Australian Freshwater Fishes Biology and Management*. John R. Merrick, Macquarie University North Ryde, NSW. Australia.

Prokop F. (2000) *Australian Fish Guide*. Australian Fishing Network, South Croydon, Australia.

Williams W. D. (1980) *Australian Freshwater Life*. Macmillan Education Australia Pty. Ltd. South Melbourne, Australia.

INDEX

INDEX CONT.